Discovering Tucson

A Guide to the Old Pueblo... and Beyond

*By Carolyn Grossman
and Suzanne Myal*

Fiesta
Publishing

Tucson, Arizona
1996

Discovering Tucson,
A Guide to the Old Pueblo...and Beyond

by Carolyn Grossman and Suzanne Myal

Copyright © 1996 Fiesta Publishing
Fiesta Publishing, P.O. Box 65106, Tucson, AZ 85718-5106

Printed in U.S.A.

Library of Congress Catalog Card Number: 95-61903
First Printing 1996
Second Printing 1996
ISBN 0-9643613-0-2

10 9 8 7 6 5 4 3 2 1

Softcover $14.95

Book Design: Godat/Jonczyk
Editing: Brandy K. Poirier
Front Cover Photo: Art Clifton
Back Cover Photo Inserts:
Boots: Art Clifton
Pima County Courthouse: Julia Anderson
San Xavier Mission: Julia Anderson
Prickly Pear Cactus: Ed Armstrong
Tucson Museum of Art Mural: Ed Armstrong
Cover Background Photo: Jeff Smith

Acknowledgements

This guide was created with the assistance and encouragement of many people. A big thanks goes to our writers and researchers, Leslie Poirier and Mark Poirier, without whom this book would not have been possible. We extend special thanks also to Michael Pollock, who stepped in toward the end to do some writing, and contributed hours and hours of computer work. Also thanks to Brandy Poirier, who not only edited for us, but also gave us lots of support and graciously helped us organize this book in a logical fashion. We'd also like to thank Todd Grayson for his contribution on rock climbing, Jeff Poirier for his writing on area hikes, Heidi Baldwin for her help with shopping, Julie Castro for her work on Nogales and her computer and marketing assistance, and Ron and Judy Reich for inspiring us and educating us on the ins and outs of self-publishing. And, to all those who have been instrumental in bringing this book to completion, and in helping us retain our sanity through it all, we are deeply grateful:

John and Tania Messina
David and Nancy Poirier
Jeff Jonczyk
Ken Godat
Herb, Jonathan, and Michael Grossman
and Mick Myal

A Note to Our Readers:

The hospitality industry – including restaurants, lodging, shops, and attractions – is, by nature, changeable. Hours, locations, prices, and owners can all vary over time, and some unfortunate establishments close altogether. The information in this guide is accurate as of the time of printing, but when in doubt, we recommend that you call ahead to verify the details of a place you wish to visit.

Contents

Introduction 8

History 12
Historic Downtown 14
El Presidio Fortress and District 16
Barrio Historico District 19
Armory Park Historic District 21

Attractions 24
Arizona-Sonora Desert Museum 25
Old Tucson Studios 28
Reid Park Zoo 29
Sabino Canyon 30
Tohono Chul Park 32
De Grazia's Gallery in the Sun 34
Mission San Xavier del Bac 36
Colossal Cave 38
Biosphere 2 40
International Wildlife Museum 41
Arizona Historical Society Museum 42
Arizona State Museum 42
Pima Air and Space Museum 43
Titan Missile Museum 45
Kitt Peak 46
Flandrau Science Center and Planetarium 48
Center for Creative Photography 49
University of Arizona Museum of Art 49
Tucson Museum of Art 50
Tucson Children's Museum 51
Tucson Botanical Gardens 52
Old Pueblo Trolley 54

Restaurants   56

Mexican Fare	57
Southwestern and Innovative Cuisine	59
Steakhouses and BBQ Spots	63
Grills	64
Continental Cuisine	67
Italian Cuisine	69
French, Spanish, and Greek Cuisine	71
Asian Cuisine	73
Vegetarian Fare	74
Cafés and Coffee Houses	74
Fast Food	76

Lodging   78

Resorts	79
Hotels	85
Bed and Breakfast Inns	88
Dude Ranches	94

Shopping   98

Ethnic Arts and Decor	99
Western Boots and Attire	104
Outdoor Gear	105
Bookstores	106
Music	109
Antiques and Collectibles	110
Thrift Stores	111
Second-Hand and Resale Boutiques	113
Miscellaneous	114

Arts & Entertainment 118

Downtown Saturday Night	119
Bars and Nightclubs	120
Honky Tonks and Western Clubs	122
Casinos	123
Family Fun	124
Theater	126
Dance	129
Music	130
Art Galleries	132
Murals	134

Day Trips 136

Tombstone	138
Bisbee	141
Tubac and Tumacacori	144
Patagonia	147
Sonoita	150
Amerind Foundation and Museum	151
Chiricahua National Monument/Wilderness	153
Willcox	154
Ghost Towns	156
Coronado National Memorial	158
Fort Huachuca	158
Mt. Lemmon	160
Nogales – Sonora, Mexico	162
Puerto Peñasco/Rocky Point – Sonora, Mexico	165

Outdoor Activities 170

Golf	171
Saguaro National Park West and East	177
Horseback Riding	180
Hiking	181
Birding	184
Santa Cruz River and Rillito River Parks	188
Biking	189
Rock Climbing	197
Skiing	201

Tours 202

Maps

The State of Arizona	10
Tucson and Surrounding Area	11
Historic Districts	15
El Presido Fortress and District	16
Barrio Historico District	20
Armory Park Historic District	21
Attractions: University Area	54
Attractions: West of Tucson	55
Attractions: North of Tucson	55
Shopping: Congress Street/Downtown	116
Shopping: Fourth Avenue	117
Shopping: Campbell Avenue	117
Day Trips from Tucson	137
Ghost Towns	157

Annual Events 206

Index 220

Writing this book was an easy task – it's easy to be enthusiastic about Tucson, and it was fun revisiting our favorite museums, stores, and restaurants, and discovering new ones. Tucsonans are extremely proud of their city, and many of the places in this book are favorite "secret spots" passed on to us by people we met in the course of our research. We learned a lot about Tucson along the way, and most of what we learned added to our appreciation of both the city and the extraordinary natural environment that surrounds it. The result is this book – *Discovering Tucson, A Guide to the Old Pueblo… and Beyond* – for which we've done the legwork required to help you chart an easy course through this diverse and distinctive region.

So that you'll enjoy your trip as much as possible, it's important to know a bit about Tucson's climate, and to come prepared to be comfortable. Tucson enjoys about 300 days of sunshine each year; winter temperatures are an average of 65°F by day, and 38°F at night. Summers are hot – with the mercury rising into the 90s and 100s through much of June, July and August. Due to Tucson's exceptionally low humidity, however, these high temperatures are more pleasant than you might expect.

Late summer brings the monsoon season, with its spectacular electrical storms and warm thundershowers. These monsoons come just in time to provide welcome rains and relief from the heat for the desert plants, animals, and near-roasted Tucsonans. More than half of the area's annual rainfall – approximately 11 inches total – falls between the months of July and September.

Throughout the year, but especially in the summer, wide-brimmed hats, sunglasses, and sunscreen provide vital protection from the Tucson sun. Light clothing in cotton and linen is a warm-weather favorite among both visitors and residents, and preferred footwear ranges from tennis shoes to canvas loafers to sandals of all types. In the winter months, you're wise to take a layered approach to dressing for the day, as mid-afternoon temperatures may soar into the 80s, then plunge down to 30°F with the sunset.

Set in a desert valley that's surrounded by mountains, Tucson has an elevation of 2,400 feet, and is 1,300 feet higher than the city of Phoenix.

Unlike many cities, Tucson takes a relaxed approach to dressing for dinner, arts events, and evening entertainment. So, while you might want to bring a bit of dressy attire, you'll feel right at home in your casual clothing in most of Tucson's restaurants, theaters, and clubs. In a climate such as this one, comfort is king!

In both its urban and natural areas, Tucson's landscape offers a never-ending tapestry of fascination. There is always another secret shop to discover, mountain path to be followed, delicious meal to be savored, story to be told. Our goal in creating this book is to provide an informative and comprehensive guide to help you to get the most out of Tucson – to make it your own – whether you're staying just a few days or for several months. Explore, investigate, and have a wonderful time discovering Tucson.

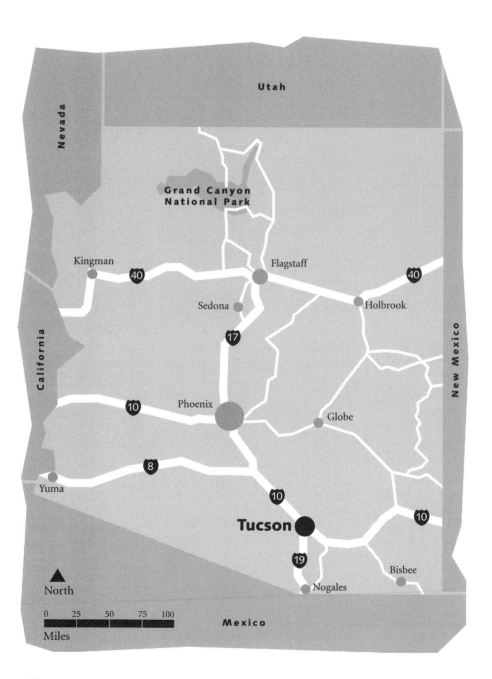

Tucson and Surrounding Area

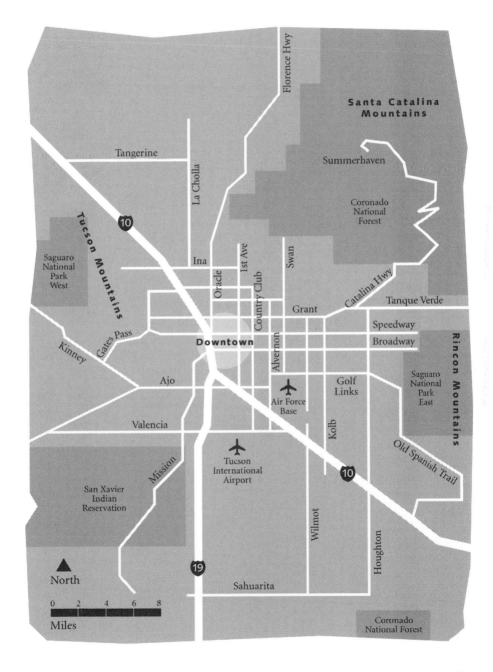

Florence Hwy

Santa Catalina Mountains

Tangerine

Summerhaven

La Cholla

Coronado National Forest

Tucson Mountains

Saguaro National Park West

Ina

Oracle

1st Ave

Country Club

Swan

Catalina Hwy

Tanque Verde

Grant

Downtown

Speedway

Broadway

Gates Pass

Kinney

Alvernon

Rincon Mountains

Ajo

Golf Links

Saguaro National Park East

Air Force Base

Kolb

Valencia

Old Spanish Trail

Mission

Tucson International Airport

San Xavier Indian Reservation

Wilmot

Houghton

▲
North

0 2 4 6 8
Miles

Sahuarita

Coronado National Forest

As is true in many cities, the color and complexity of Tucson can be clearly traced to its past, but unlike many cities, the myriad influences that have shaped Tucson remain a vital part of its existence today. Tucson's diverse heritage continues to thrive, as the Native American, Spanish, Mexican, and pioneer influences are honored by all, and are never devalued or forgotten.

The first residents of the Tucson area, the Hohokam (a Pima Indian word meaning "those who have vanished"), farmed along the Santa Cruz River as early as the first century A.D. Little is known about this primitive tribe, which vanished mysteriously long before the Spanish first explored the area in the 1500s, but you can learn more about the Hohokam by visiting the Arizona State Museum, listed in the *Attractions* section of this book.

When Padre Eusebio Francisco Kino, a Jesuit missionary from Spain, visited the area in 1692, he found the land occupied by Pima and Sobaipuri Indians. The Pima lived at the foot of Sentinel Peak (now known as "A" Mountain) in a village called "Stjukshone." The word roughly translates to "spring at the foot of a black mountain," and later evolved into "Tucson."

Tucson's "A" Mountain has come to symbolize school spirit for the University of Arizona. Every year since 1915, the giant "A" on the eastern face of the mountain has been whitewashed by freshmen students as part of the annual autumn Homecoming celebration.

Spanish soldiers built the walled Presidio of San Augustin de Tucson during the 1770s and 1780s to provide refuge to travelers and residents. The fort had adobe walls

Tucson is the oldest continually inhabited settlement in the U.S.

that were 12 feet high and 70 feet wide. A small portion of the original Presidio – dubbed "the Old Pueblo" by early settlers – has been well preserved, and can be seen on the second floor of the Pima County Courthouse building in downtown Tucson.

The Spanish flag was the first of four to be flown over the city. Tucson became part of Mexico when that country gained its independence from Spain in 1821. Old Glory has flown over this land since the area was claimed by the U.S. as part of the 1854 Gadsen Purchase, except for a brief period during the Civil War, when Confederate soldiers raised their flag.

Tucson is Arizona's second largest city, with a population of about 700,000.

Still a Territory, Tucson earned its reputation as a wild Western town in the 1860s. The Butterfield stage coach line delivered ranchers, farmers, and fugitives to the area, gunfights were common, and a six-shooter was a vital accessory for those considering a walk about town. Today, the Wild West atmosphere of Tucson is recreated at Old Tucson, a fully operational movie studio and theme park located west of downtown. Tucsonans are proud of their Western heritage, and it lives on in the local honky-tonks and rodeo grounds.

Real growth occurred in Tucson when the first train arrived in 1880, bringing settlers in search of land and gold-seeking miners. Shortly thereafter the area's population soared to more than 7,000. Tucson's tradition of higher education began in 1891, when the Arizona Territorial University opened on land donated by a saloonkeeper and a couple of gamblers. By some accounts, this seemingly generous transaction was actually a hasty settlement of a sizable gambling debt. On Valentine's Day in 1912, the Territory of Arizona was ushered into the realm of the United States.

Tucson's development remained slow but steady until World War II, when Davis Monthan Air Force Base became an official U.S. military post, and the city's population swelled

Courtesy of AZ Historical Society

South Meyer Avenue in 1904.

dramatically with servicemen and B-17 bomber pilots. Many of those who trained at Davis Monthan found the area's unique climate irresistible, and relocated to Tucson with their families following the war. Davis Monthan continues to be a vital part of Tucson, providing employment for local citizens and attracting thousands of visitors annually. A great way to learn about Davis Monthan's history is to head down to the Pima Air and Space Museum and take a look at the hundreds of artifacts on display. Information can be found on this museum in the *Attractions* section.

Despite the presence of Davis Monthan, Tucson did not develop into a simple military town. Other industries, such as copper mining, tourism and agriculture, have also been thoroughly developed. And, as the University of Arizona now enrolls more than 40,000 students annually, Tucson has become widely known as a great university town as well.

Today, Tucson's population is comprised of a wide array of students, young couples, maturing families, health-conscious senior citizens, and seasonal residents – people with varying interests, backgrounds, and lifestyles. What these diverse individuals have in common is a deep appreciation for the city's fascinating environment – both urban and wild – its absorbing history, and ever-emerging culture.

Historic Downtown

There are three distinct historical areas in downtown Tucson: the El Presidio, Barrio Historico, and Armory Park districts. Each has its own unique features and history. We've provided a brief overview of the districts' most important sites, but if you'd like to gain a more comprehensive understanding of historic downtown, we suggest that you take part in one of the fun and informative tours listed below.

The Tucson Museum of Art leads guided tours of their Historic Block every Wednesday and Thursday starting at 11 a.m. from November through April. Call 520-624-2333 for reservations or information. The Arizona Historic Society also conducts guided tours – about two hours in length – every Saturday from October through April. Call 520-622-0956 for details. You can also pickup a self-guided walking tour of Tucson's History from the historic sites Society or the Tucson Visitor's Bureau at 130 S. Scott Avenue (1-800-638-8350).

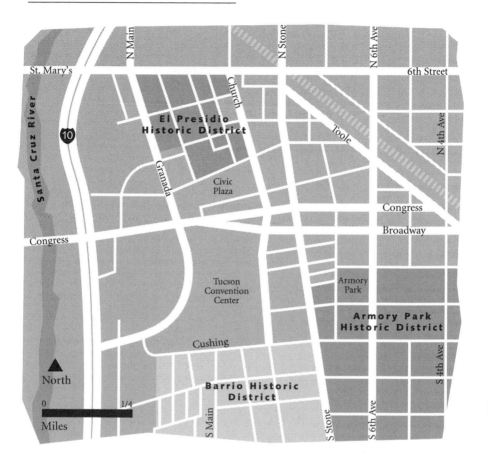

El Presidio Historic District

Armory Park Historic District

Barrio Historic District

Tucson Convention Center

Civic Plaza

Armory Park

Santa Cruz River

St. Mary's

6th Street

Congress

Broadway

Congress

Cushing

Church

Granada

Toole

N Main

N Stone

N 6th Ave

N 4th Ave

S Main

S Stone

S 6th Ave

S 4th Ave

North

0   1/4

Miles

El Presidio Fortress and District

In 1776, El Presidio fortress was relocated from the town of Tubac to Tucson in order to protect the area that was then known as the Santa Cruz Valley. The fort had a huge mesquite door that was locked securely at night, and in times of danger. While the fort walls are no longer standing, you can take a look at a piece of the once-formidable barrier at the Pima County Courthouse.

While the El Presidio District extends beyond the zone that was once enclosed by the walls of the fortress, all of the sites we've listed below are located inside the old fortress boundaries, and are within easy walking distance of one another. The El Presidio District was home to much of Tucson's upper echelon during the 1880s, several of whom lived in the homes listed below.

El Presidio Fortress and District

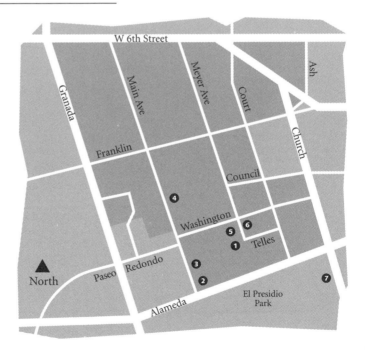

① La Casa Cordova

175 N. Meyer Ave.

One of the oldest houses in the area, this 1848 home was named for its last resident, Maria Navarette Cordova. The 5-room, "L" shaped adobe structure has been restored to its original style, and is now the home of the Mexican Heritage Museum. The small museum has a display of recently found artifacts, and a small-scale replica of the original Presidio. If you're here during the months of November through March, you will also enjoy Maria Luisa Teña's display of *Nacimientos,* or, nativity scenes. This local resident and honorary docent has been creating elaborate Christmas scenes inspired by rural Mexico and the Old and New Testament since 1978.

② Edward Nye Fish House

120 N. Main Ave.

The Edward Nye Fish House was built in 1867 for the wealthy businessman and politician for whom it is named. Originally from Massachusetts, Edward Fish started a hardware store in California before making his way to Tucson, where he opened a successful general store. Fish's wife, Maria Wakefield, was a school teacher, and was instrumental in establishing the first territorial university.

The house is known to have been used for many social events, including several notable weddings. The adobe walls on the house are an amazing 2 feet thick, and the 15-foot beamed ceiling is lined with saguaro cactus rib supports. It will soon house the Campbell Gallery, a collection of Western Art put on display by the Tucson Museum of Art.

③ Stevens House

150 N. Main Ave.

Hiram Sanford Stevens first came to Tucson in 1852 after a stint with the Army, and ultimately became a wealthy cattle rancher by selling hay and beef to the Army itself. After three years in Tucson, Stevens married the 16-year-old Petra Santa Cruz, and moved back to his native state of Vermont in 1861. The Stevens returned to Tucson because Petra did not adjust well to life in Vermont. It was at this time, in 1865, that the all-adobe Stevens House was built.

In 1893, a severe drought killed most of Stevens' cattle and ruined his business. Distraught and depressed, Stevens shot Petra, and then killed himself. Ironically, Petra was completely unscathed, as the bullet from Stevens' gun ricocheted off the large Spanish comb in her hair and barely grazed her scalp. Currently, the site serves as home of Janos restaurant, listed in the *Restaurant* section of this book.

4 The Corbett House

257 N. Main Ave.

In 1880, J. Knox Corbett moved from South Carolina to Tucson. A true entrepreneur, Corbett eventually opened up the Corbett Lumber Company, and served as mayor and postmaster in Tucson just after the turn of the century. Through his lumber company, and a series of wide investments in ranches and stage lines, Corbett became one of Tucson's most successful men.

The Corbett House was designed by the popular Tucson architect, D.H. Holmes, and was built in 1907. Unlike most of the historic homes in this area, the house is constructed of brick, and has a red clay tile roof that is particular to Mission Revival style buildings.

5 Romero House

101 W. Washington St.

Leonardo Romero was an excellent carpenter who participated in the construction of the St. Augustine Cathedral, and the restoration of the San Xavier Mission. He was the first resident of this house on Meyer Avenue, which is believed to have been built in 1868.

Outside, you can see where parts of the original adobe walls have been replaced with brick, and, on the Washington Street side of the building, where a gabled roof now covers the home's first flat mud roof. The site is currently being used by the Tucson Museum of Art School, and is not open to the public.

⑥ Old Town Artisans

186 N. Meyer Ave.

This old adobe marketplace offers Mexican, Native American, and Western arts and crafts created by more than 150 artists. In addition to picking up some nice gifts, you can take a break from your tour over a snack in the lovely courtyard cafe. See the *Shopping* section for more information.

⑦ Pima County Courthouse

115 N. Church St.

Although not technically situated within the El Presidio District, the courthouse is located in the area that was once the El Presidio fort. In fact, on the first floor of the courthouse is where you'll see one of the last remaining portions of the original Presidio wall. Built in 1869 as a small adobe structure, the courthouse was reconstructed on the same site as a much larger, Colonial style-building in 1927.

You may recognize the east facade of the building as the location in which Barbara Streisand and Kris Kristofferson were married in the movie, *A Star is Born.* Many scenes from the television series, *Petrocelli,* were also filmed here. The beautiful tiled dome that crowns the courthouse incorporates Moorish, Spanish, and Southwestern architectural features.

Barrio Historico District

Known in the 1800s as "Barrio Libre" because of loosely enforced law in the neighborhood, the Barrio Historico reflects its heritage in the rows of Sonoran-style adobe houses that make up this district.

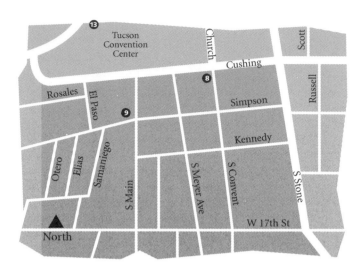

8 Cushing Street Bar and Grill

343 S. Meyer Ave.

Built more than 100 years ago, this building contains an old country store and the Joseph Ferin Home. The building is named after Howard Cushing, a popular army hero, and has many old photos of the surrounding neighborhood area. For more information, see the *Arts & Entertainment* section.

9 Wishing Shrine

S. Main Ave.

This is the only known shrine in the United States that is dedicated to sinners, making it a unique place to visit. Legend tells of a young herder, Juan Oliveras, who was killed in a lovers' triangle. Because his body was buried in unconsecrated ground, the religious people of the town lit candles at this spot and prayed for his soul. The story has evolved and become more widely known over the years and as a result, many light candles here in hopes that their wishes will come true. According to the legend, if the candle you light stays aflame all night, your wish will be granted.

It was when the railroad came through in 1880 that Tucson finally began to emerge as more of a city than a town. Many of those who came by rail ended up living in what is now the Armory Park Historic District.

Armory Park Historic District

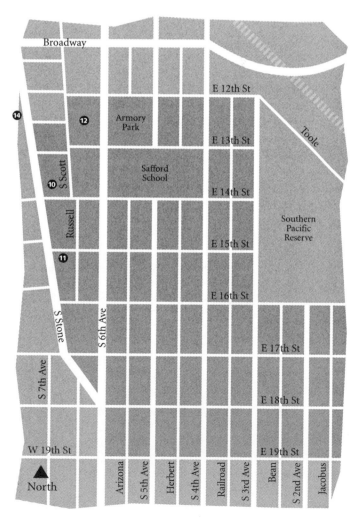

The homes in the Armory Park district reflect the evolution of architectural styles that took place around the turn of the century. As part of a movement away from the Spanish designs that had prevailed, the boxy, Sonoran-style adobe houses were "updated" with wooden roofs and porches that were more commonly found in the East. As new homes were built in the area, this more "refined" look became even more widespread.

⑩ Temple of Music and Art

330 S. Scott Ave.

Now the home of the Arizona Theater Company, this refurbished 1927 building was a movie and stage theater in its earlier days. In fact, it was here that Tucson's first "talkies," moving pictures with sound, were shown in the later 1920s. The Temple enjoyed some restoration in 1976, more in the early '90s, and today contains a 603-seat main theater, a 90-seat cabaret, art gallery, and gift shop. In addition, the newly relocated Bailey & Bailey Café is adjacent to the Temple, and serves dinner on performance nights.

⑪ El Fronterizo

471 S. Stone Ave.

In 1878, Carlos Y. Velasco moved into this building and turned it into a printing office for a Spanish-language newspaper. During the recent reconstruction of El Fronterizo, some of the original handset type that was used to create the paper was found under the floorboards.

⑫ Tucson Children's Museum

200 S. Sixth Ave.

Originally established as part of the national library program supported by Andrew Carnegie, this 1901 building was designed by architect Henry Trost, and currently serves as the Tucson Children's Museum (see the listing under *Attractions* for more information on the museum).

Noteworthy Sites Near the Historic Districts

⑬ Sosa-Carrillo-Frémont House Museum

151 S. Granada Ave.

The Sosa-Carrillo-Frémont House Museum is the only original adobe building left from the barrio neighborhood that once existed where the Tucson Convention Center Complex now resides. Originally built in 1858, it was enlarged in 1866 and is named after those who resided in the building throughout its long history. Among those notable residents was John C. Frémont, the well-known explorer and the fifth territorial governor of Arizona. Now a branch of the Arizona Historical Society, the museum is furnished in 1880s decor and features rotating displays that present various aspects of territorial life.

Refer to Barrio Historico map on page 20.

⑭ Saint Augustine Cathedral

192 S. Stone Ave.

The cathedral, modeled after the Cathedral of Queretero in Mexico, was constructed in 1896. In 1920, it was extensively renovated and enhanced with the addition of lovely stained glass windows and an impressive sandstone facade. The cathedral was further remodeled in 1967 to expand the seating area to accommodate more parishioners.

A 1900 painting of Our Lady of Guadalupe, donated from a church in Mexico City, hangs on one wall, and, above the church door is a statue of St. Augustine and symbols of the Arizona desert: the horned toad, the saguaro, and the yucca. Every Sunday at 8 a.m. there is a Mariachi Mass that visitors are welcome to attend.

For more information on the historic districts of the Old Pueblo, you can purchase a copy of Harry and Mary Cuming's book, *Yesterday's Tucson Today,* at one of Tucson's many local bookstores.

Refer to Armory Park map on page 21.

Tucson has a wide range of fascinating and edifying attractions that will give you an inside look at the environment, his- tory, and culture that make Southeastern Arizona distinct from any other region in the world. Get a close-up look at indigenous wildlife, investigate the area's natural and military history, explore the Arizona night sky, and feast your eyes on the spectacular work of renowned artists from the Southwest and beyond. At the end of this section, you'll find a list of Tucson's most popular attractions grouped geographically, to help you plan a convenient itinerary for sightseeing in the area.

Icon Guide

🍴	*Food, snacks and refreshments*
🍷	*Beer, wine or cocktails*
☕	*Coffee and hot drinks*
👓	*Sunglasses recommended*
💧	*Bring water*
🎩	*Hat recommended*
🪑	*Picnic tables available*
🎁	*Gift Shop*
👟	*Hiking shoes recommended*

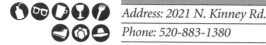

Arizona-Sonora Desert Museum

Address: *2021 N. Kinney Rd.*

Phone: *520-883-1380*

Hours: *Open every day of the year: October-February 8:30 a.m. to 5 p.m.; March-September 7:30 a.m. to 6 p.m.*

Admission: *Adults (ages 13 and older) $8.95, Children 6-12 $1.75, Children under 6 free. Admission covers all exhibits. Special rates for groups of 20 or more.*

The Arizona-Sonora Desert Museum has been rated as one of America's 10 top zoos by Parade, *a magazine with a national readership of 65 million.*

Don't be fooled by the name – the Arizona-Sonora Desert Museum is not your typical museum. You won't find dusty artifacts or be guided down long halls lined with baroque paintings. Most of the exhibits here are living, breathing individuals who make their homes in the Sonoran Desert. Touted by the *New York Times* as "...the most distinctive zoo in the United States," the Desert Museum is an attraction that Tucsonans themselves visit time after time. It was founded in 1952, and remains a private, not-for-profit organization whose growth and operations are financed entirely by admissions, memberships, and contributions. The museum's collection of animals, plants, and geology gives you the opportunity to learn about every aspect of the Sonoran Desert, from its varied reptilian life to its minerals and precious stones.

As you enter the museum grounds, you'll be treated to a lizard display in which various reptiles bask on rocks and munch unsuspecting bugs. Inside the park, more than 200 different living animals and 1,200 kinds of plants inhabit hundreds of indoor and outdoor exhibits that educate and entertain.

Docent with visitors at the Arizona-Sonora Desert Museum.

Courtesy of Arizona-Sonora Desert Museum

The Earth Science Center allows you to cool off as you wander through simulated caves and learn about our planet's geological history and life in the dark. The Loop Trail within the exhibit gives you an opportunity to test your skills at basic spelunking. The trail is 75 feet of "low ceilings, steep climbs, rough footing, and extremely tight passages." From one vantage point on the trail, you can see a pool beneath the stalagmites where colorful tiger salamanders swim freely.

Another favorite exhibit is the Riparian Habitat, which houses a pack of playful otters. The otters, as well as other aquatic mammals and native fish, are visible through a special underwater viewing window. In the mornings, you may even have a chance to see the otters being fed from the area above.

For bird lovers, the museum offers numerous exhibits that feature over 300 feathered individuals that live in the Sonoran Desert, including countless species of hummingbirds. In the outdoor hummingbird exhibit you can see members of many different species buzzing and feeding. Some will stop and hover curiously within inches of your face, and, during nest-building season, these plucky birds may even try to steal loose threads from your clothing. Special bird-watching tours are given daily; the museum can provide you with a tour schedule.

The museum's new Grasslands exhibit features spirited prairie dogs who pose for pictures and chase one another through the network of tunnels and holes known as their "town." The exhibit also features a replica of an archeological site – with bones and fossils dating back to the Pleistocene period – and provides a complete history of the Sonoran Desert grasslands. Glassed-in displays give you a close-up view of cross sections of termite colonies and rattlesnakes in their natural habits.

A lizard basking on a rock at the Museum.

Courtesy of Arizona-Sonora Desert Museum

It's wise to schedule your visit to the Desert Museum as early in the day as possible – especially in the summer months – and plan to stay for at least two hours. Mornings at the museum are less crowded, it's cooler, and the animals are more active. Be sure to take advantage of the knowledgeable docents who station themselves throughout the grounds and give special presentations. Docents also give tours of the museum, explaining everything from the growth of cacti to how a rattlesnake's rattle works. Call for specific tour times.

The Desert Museum is impeccably maintained and offers a wide range of refreshments. Picnicking is not allowed on museum grounds, but there are picnic areas in nearby Tucson Mountain Park. All indoor exhibits are cooled – offering welcome relief from the heat in the summer months. The new Ironwood Terraces offers Mexican, American, and vegetarian cuisine at reasonable prices. Try the prickly-pear tea or the

Southwestern Grilled Cheese. Domestic and Mexican beers are also available. All exhibits are wheelchair accessible and wheelchairs and strollers are available free of charge. The extensive gift shop offers everything from cactus jelly to Native American literature.

Located 14 miles west of downtown in Tucson Mountain Park, the Arizona-Sonora Desert Museum is easily accessible. The drive from downtown is a scenic one, and you'll enjoy the spectacular views of the Tucson Mountains no matter which route you take. For the best views, drive through Gates Pass and wind down the western side of the mountains.

Old Tucson Studios

Address: *201 S. Kinney Rd.*	
Phone: *520-883-0100*	
Hours: *Daily from 9 a.m. until the last gunfight at 7:30 p.m.*	
Admission: *Adults $11.95, children ages 4-11 $7.95, children 3 and under free. After 5 p.m. admission for adults drops to $7.95. Guided tours are $3.*	

Old Tucson Studios is known as "Hollywood in the Desert." More than 200 movies, commercials, documentaries, and television shows have been filmed here since it was built as a set for the movie Arizona *in 1939.*

Note: *On April 24, 1995, a major fire engulfed most of Old Tucson Studios. While there were no serious injuries, the fire destroyed most of the park and movie sets. The park is currently closed for repair, and has given no definite reopening date. Call the above number for more current information before visiting, as the situation at Old Tucson will probably have improved by the time you read this.*

Old Tucson Studios was originally built as a set for *Arizona*, a 1939 Columbia Motion Pictures production starring William Holden and Jean Arthur. Since then, it has served as the set for hundreds of movies, television shows, and commercials. It was along the dusty streets of Old Tucson that John Wayne walked in *Rio Lobo* and Emilio Estevez herded cattle in *Young Guns II*. Today, it is quite possible to

Courtesy of Old Tucson Studios

The Old Tucson train ride.

get a peek behind the scenes of the filming of any number of productions. Call Old Tucson for details about what may be in production.

 Old Tucson is more than just a studio set; it is also an exciting theme park that has the majestic Tucson Mountains as a backdrop. You might turn a corner to witness a shoot-out or a bar brawl as stunt men showcase their talents throughout the day, then take a ride through the Iron

You will encounter cowboys and lots of action at Old Tucson Studios.

Door Mine where you'll be heckled by skeletons and other frightful beings. For young children, the Silverlake Park area offers various amusements, including the Rio Bravo canoe ride and the Iron Pony hand cars, as well as a video arcade and a shooting gallery. Also of interest is the Simmons Gun Museum, which houses over 1,000 weapons from the Old West and all over the world, an extensive Firehouse Exhibit, and a new Kachina Museum.

Because no two visits to Old Tucson are the same, Arizonans continue stop by the studios. In fact, 25% of the daily visitors are from Arizona, 50% are from the rest of the United States, and the remaining 25% visit from other countries. Depending on the timing of your trip, you may be lucky enough to see a rodeo or participate in "Nightfall," a Halloween adventure that takes place in October of each year. Call Old Tucson for further information about special events.

Reid Park Zoo

Address: Enter off 22nd between Country Club & Randolph Way

Phone: 520-791-4022

Hours: Daily from 9 a.m. to 4 p.m.
Open all holidays except Christmas.

Admission: Adults $3.50, senior citizens $2.50, children 5-14 75¢, children 4 and under free.

This unique zoo is located within the city limits of Tucson and is home to over 400 exotic animals. Many of these are endangered species that are involved in captive breeding programs. These programs have been designed to protect and monitor such rare animals as the small clawed otter, Siberian tiger, white rhinoceros, Grey's zebra, lion-tailed macaque, and Bali mynah. The Reid Park Zoo is especially noted for its captive breeding program for the giant anteater, which is the most successful in the world. Examples of species that have been saved by similar programs include the American bison and the whooping crane.

The zoo has many open enclosures that allow close-up views of the animals. Although you'll see the most activity early in the morning, some of the animals are busy throughout the day. The giraffes, antelope, and jovial elephants tend to be the most active of the larger mammals. Other popular enclosures include the polar bears' and primates'.

If you work up an appetite during your visit, stop by the zoo's shady snack bar for a sandwich or burger – they also serve a good veggie burger. Outside the zoo, Reid Park offers several different picnic options.

More than just a zoo, Reid Park is considered one of Tucson's premier parks. It features swimming pools, tennis courts, horseshoe pits, a formal rose garden, and two 18-hole golf courses. Located near the picnic facilities is a duck pond that's home to several feathered friends.

It's not recommended that you feed these waterfowl, but since some people do, they can be aggressive if they think you come bearing snacks. For this reason, it is wise to accompany small children when they venture toward the pond.

Sabino Canyon

Address: 5900 N. Sabino Canyon Rd.

Phone: 520-749-2861 Sabino Canyon Tours, Inc.
Information and tour schedule; 520-749-2327. Moonlight reservations/group tour rates. Narrated tram rides every 30 minutes.

Hours: Open daily from dawn to dusk. Tram rides are offered from 9 a.m. to 4:30 p.m. During the summer, rides are held M-F 9 a.m. to 4 p.m.

Admission: Free. Seven Falls tram ride: Adults $3, children $1.25; Sabino Falls tram ride: Adults $5, children 3-12 $2.

Sabino Canyon has been one of southern Arizona's most beautiful and accessible canyons for thousands of years. Traces of Native American life, specifically the Hohokam, have been found throughout the canyon. Small holes in stones that were used to grind mesquite beans and hunting tools can still be seen today by hikers, picnickers, swimmers, birdwatchers, and runners, all of whom find the canyon to be a perfect place for their activities. Once threatened by the construction of a dam, Sabino Canyon has remained home to a wide variety of cacti and animal life. A Visitors Center, a wide variety of trails, and a shuttle service allow guests to become familiar with life in the Sonoran Desert.

For the novice hiker, a short nature trail begins right next to the Visitors Center. Various trails loop through Lower Sabino Canyon as well, and you can take the shuttle to even more trailheads.

About two and a half miles from a designated shuttle stop is Seven Falls, a spectacular series of cascades and swimming holes. The Seven Falls Trail is probably one of Tucson's most popular hikes because it's relatively easy, only about two miles in each direction, and it crosses back and forth over a creek. It also offers amazing views of Bear Canyon. Plunging into the swimming holes below the falls is an exhilarating way to cool off, depending on the time of year and the weather.

Less crowded than the Seven Falls Trail are the Telephone Line and Esperero Canyon Trails. Both are popular with hikers and provide dramatic views. The Telephone Line Trail, which was cut in 1911, leads you along the steep eastern slope of the canyon. Its name is inspired by the old telephone poles that line parts of the trail. Although the trail runs parallel to the shuttle's route into the canyon, it travels along a high ridge, and is far removed from the road. The trail gains a lot of elevation in a short distance and after about five or six miles it connects to the road at the last shuttle stop. It is possible to return to the parking lot by turning around or heading down the road. You may also want to continue up to Mt. Lemmon, if you're well-prepared for an additional 14 miles of rigorous hiking.

The Esperero Canyon Trail is also one that gains substantial elevation in a short distance. It departs in a northwest direction and offers spectacular views of Rattlesnake Canyon and Bird Canyon and eventually leads to Esperero Canyon itself. This is a challenging hike.

Tucson has a surprisingly large variety of birds, animals and plants. The desert vegetation is lush, with many mesquite trees, palo verde trees and cottonwoods. This is due, in part, to the dramatic variations in climate that occur with changes in elevation.

Hikers crossing one of the many bridges in Sabino Canyon.

Ed Armstrong

In the winter, spring, fall, or even during the morning hours in summer, the Sabino Canyon Recreation Area is perfect for picnickers. Water runs through the canyon throughout the year, but spring is the preferred season for swimmers to visit, when the cool pools fill to their capacity. April is the best time of year to see cacti in bloom, but some continue to bear flowers into the summer.

Because of the creeks that run through the recreation area, wildlife is varied and abundant throughout the year. Even from the trams, visitors may be lucky enough to see Big Horn sheep, javelinas and mule deer. Swimmers and waders may feel a few nibbles from brazen minnows and spot amazingly camouflaged gray frogs. More than 250 species of birds, including the roadrunner, can be seen year round.

In addition to the regular schedule of shuttle service, Sabino Canyon Tours, Inc. offers moonlight rides three nights per month from April to June and September through December. Call ahead for reservations.

Tohono Chul Park

Address: 7366 N. Paseo del Norte
(First stoplight on Ina west of Oracle)

Phone: Information – 520-575-8468;
Administration – 520-742-6455; Tea Room – 520-797-1711

Hours: Park grounds – Daily 7 a.m. to sunset;
Exhibit House – M-Sat 9:30 a.m. to 5 p.m. and Sun 11 a.m. to 5 p.m.; Tea Room – Daily 8 a.m. to 5 p.m.;
Administration – M-F 8:30 a.m. to 5 p.m.

Admission: Free; $2 donation appreciated for featured exhibit.

In the Tohono O'odham language, *Tohono Chul* means "desert corner." This beautiful 37-acre oasis on the northwest side of Tucson was designed with one major goal: to promote the preservation of delicate arid regions by encouraging the use of native plants and minimal water in landscaping. It's easy to forget how precious water is to the Sonoran Desert's survival! More than 400 native species of exquisite desert plants come together here to create the living museum of Tohono Chul Park.

The park was originally an estate held by an eastern family. As Tucson began to grow northward, owners Richard and Jean Wilson recognized the importance of preserving their pristine land in its natural state for the community's long-term enjoyment. It followed that in 1985, Tohono Chul was formally dedicated as a not-for-profit park and opened to the public free of charge.

The park is complete with a system of inner and outer trails that is extremely accessible and suitable for all ages. The inner trail system connects the park's current exhibits, and the outer loop will take you on an extensive tour of the natural desert. Along this path, you will encounter plants from Arizona, southern Texas, and northern Mexico. There are also majestic saguaros and palo verdes along the trail, both of which are native to southern Arizona. The Succulent Ramada is home to 100 species of water-hoarding cacti, and within the Pincushion Ramada reside several small, brightly blooming cacti.

The Demonstration Garden shows you how to carry this beauty home. Offering attractive water-saving ideas for in-home use or commercial landscaping, this garden combines desert plants, patio designs, and materials to create a comfortable – almost cooling – oasis. A simulated desert stream and grotto pond along the garden contain gila top-minnows and desert pupfish.

Another impressive garden is the Ethnobotanical Garden. It contains historical desert-adapted crops and wild plants descended from those which were cultivated by native peoples. An irrigation exhibit demonstrates the reuse of run-off water, and features a design that is easily adaptable for home use.

The Park Greenhouse contains many native and arid land plants that are for sale. The majority of them have been generated from seeds collected from vegetation on the park.

Animals thrive in this living museum as well. Several species of birds, for example, wisely choose to reside on the site. Birding tours are conducted by docents, and you can rely on the several bird stations along the trails for information and identification. Cactus wrens, cardinals, and roadrunners are the birds most frequently sighted, and you may even observe woodpeckers hammering away at or peering out of saguaros. One of the most charming of the desert birds is the Gambel's quail, which travels in a covey and usually has a few babies scurrying behind.

Most of the birds – especially the quick roadrunner – have no trouble finding dinner at the park. Tasty bugs abound and several species of lizard roam the grounds as well. The roadrunner, however, must always remain on the lookout, as many coyotes come to the grounds to seek refuge from the sprawling development of Tucson. The largest mammal that appears in the park is the collared peccary, or javelina, which can weigh up to 50 pounds. They are more apt to be seen at night, however, and are generally afraid of people. Do be cautious if you run across them with their young in tow.

Inside a 55-year-old restored adobe building is the lovely Exhibit House. Here you'll find contemporary and traditional paintings, as well as sculpture, crafts, and environmental exhibits. The library is rich in landscaping, historical, and botanical topics for those who wish to conduct research.

After completing the tour, you're likely to have worked up an appetite. Fortunately, Tohono Chul Park is complete with both a Tea Room and a Garden Café which serve delicious breakfasts, lunches, or afternoon teas. There are also two gift shops that offer crafts from Southwestern artists and imports from Central and South America and Mexico. The prices here are competitive with those you'll find at most specialty shops, and 100% of the stores' proceeds are applied toward the preservation of the magnificent Tohono Chul Park.

De Grazia's Gallery in the Sun

Address: 6300 N. Swan Rd.	
Phone: 520-299-9191	
Hours: Daily 10 a.m. to 4 p.m.	
Admission: Suggested donation only.	

If you are a fan of Ted De Grazia, or just would like to become more familiar with his distinctive works of art, the Gallery in the Sun should certainly be a part of your Tucson experience. The architecture of the gallery is as stunning as the art you'll find inside, as it was designed by the artist himself. In fact, De Grazia once lived and worked at the site that is now the Gallery in the Sun. This location was so much a part of De Grazia that his own modest grave is on the premises. If you'd like, ask a museum representative for a tour of the gallery and grounds.

Each and every room of the gallery pays tribute to this dynamic artist. His works are elegantly displayed with accompanying narratives that describe the methods he used. Permanent collections are thematically organized. One room is devoted to Padre Kino. Another is filled with works inspired by Tohono O'odham legends, including the painting entitled "The Desert Medicine Man." In this piece, a Tohono O'odham healer holding colorful feathers sits under a mesquite ramada and tries to heal a sick Native American while others look on. In another room in the gallery is "Los Niños." This famous painting – of a circle of Mexican children – was used by UNICEF to raise millions of dollars to provide emergency aid for children in need.

De Grazia's talent extended far beyond painting, and the Gallery in the Sun has several rotating exhibits that give you a larger perspective on how dynamic this artist really was. The great variety of pieces that are on display include bronzes, enamels, ceramics, stone lithographs, serigraphs, and jewelry.

In addition to the beautiful art that you would expect to find here, there are many biographical exhibits that reveal much about the artist's fascinating life, including his study under Mexican artist, Diego Rivera. In one room, you may opt to see a short video presentation or you can simply look over the several narratives and photographs for a more complete picture of De Grazia.

Adjacent to the gallery you'll find the Mission in the Sun. This little chapel was built in honor of Padre Kino and was dedicated to our Lady of Guadalupe, the patron saint of Mexico. The beautiful mission, constructed by De Grazia and his friends, has many colorful murals on its interior walls that are brilliantly illuminated by the sunlight which floods through the open roof.

The Gallery in the Sun is run by the De Grazia Art and Cultural Foundation. De Grazia created the foundation to ensure that the public would continue to be able to enjoy his beloved gallery. Although none of the works inside are available for purchase, there is a gift shop on the premises that offers a variety of items for sale.

The late
Ted De Grazia.

Courtesy of De Grazia Art & Cultural Found.

Mission San Xavier del Bac

Address: 1950 W. San Xavier Rd.

Phone: 520-294-2624

Hours: Daily from 8 a.m. to 6 p.m.

Admission: Free.

The Mission San Xavier del Bac is located on the San Xavier District of the Tohono O'odham Indian Reservation southwest of Tucson. This is one of the most photographed churches in the country and one of the last Spanish missions still serving its original Native-American parishioners. The extent of restoration efforts has earned the mission the title of "the Sistine Chapel of North America."

San Xavier del Bac, known as the "White Dove of the Desert," is one of southern Arizona's most beautiful and historic monuments. The mission was founded in 1692 by Padre Eusebio Francisco Kino, and construction of the first chapel began in 1700. The present church was built between 1783 and 1797, during the administration of Father Juan Bautista Velderrain and Father Juan Bautista Llorenz. The name of the building's architect remains a mystery, as does the reason that one of the mission's towers remains incomplete. The artisans who bedecked the building with their handiwork of statues and paintings back in the 1700s also remain nameless. Today, Mission San Xavier del Bac is still a Catholic parish in the Diocese of Tucson, with daily masses and more than 200,000 pilgrims and visitors each year.

The amazing, yet subtle blending of Moorish, Byzantine, and late Mexican Renaissance forms has given San Xavier del Bac the reputation as the finest example of Mission architecture in the United States. Its white edifice is striking against the backdrop of muted greens and browns of the Sonoran Desert, and is easily spotted from afar. The entire structure is an arrangement of domes, towers, and arches, and almost every surface on the interior has been adorned, painted, and repainted throughout the years. The mesmerizing paintings on the interior walls tell the story of Christianity, and are having their original luster returned through a restoration project that's scheduled to be completed in 1996.

Above the main door is an ornate facade that is made especially interesting by the myth that surrounds it. The facade bears the representation of a cat chasing a mouse, and, according to the legend, if the cat succeeds in catching the mouse, the world will come to an end.

To the left of the ornate main altar is the reclining statue of St. Francis Xavier. Many people from the southwestern United States and northern Mexico make special pilgrimages to this altar to light votive candles and pray for the saint's intercession. The main altar itself is considered to be the finest example of a Spanish *retable* north of Mexico.

There are many individual shrines within the grounds of the Mission, including the Chapel of the Sorrowful Mother, which houses spectacular representations of saints and martyrs. The replica of Our Lady of Lourdes Shrine was built into the Hill of the Cross to the east in 1908 in celebration of the 50th anniversary of the apparitions at Lourdes.

If you're visiting the Mission to marvel at the architecture and artwork, plan to stay for one to two hours. Masses are held Tuesday through Friday at 9 a.m., Saturday at 5:30 p.m., and on Sundays at 8, 9:30, 11 a.m., and 12:30 p.m. Take care not to disturb services if you are visiting during mass; there's plenty to see outside until the service ends. You may take photographs anywhere in or around the Mission, but please don't use a flash during services. A tape-recorded tour tells you about the history of the Mission as you explore it yourself, and ends with the peaceful music of a Tohono O'odham chorus. This tour runs every 20 minutes. Call the number above for information about special services, especially around the holidays.

The Mission is located about 10 miles south of downtown Tucson in the heart of the Tohono O'odham reservation on the banks of the Santa Cruz River. Across from the main structure is a small marketplace where the Tohono O'odham sell their wares: Native American crafts, art, and refreshments. The gift shop at the Mission is open daily from 8 a.m. to 6 p.m., and in the winter months from 9 a.m. to 5 p.m..

Mission San Xavier del Bac.

Colossal Cave

Directions: Travel east on Broadway Blvd. to Old Spanish Trail, turn right onto Old Spanish Trail, which leads directly to the cave; or take I-10 east to exit 279.

Phone: 520-647-7275

Hours: M-Sat 9 a.m. to 5 p.m., Sun and holidays 8 a.m. to 7 p.m.; Summer hours (March 16-Sept. 15) M-Sat 8 a.m. to 6 p.m., Sun and holidays 8 a.m. to 7 p.m.

Admission: Adults 17 and older $6.50, juniors 11 -16 $5, children 6-10 $3.50, infants, 5 years and younger free (with paid admission).

Colossal Cave is one of the largest dry caverns in the world. Explorers have yet to find its end.

Colossal Cave is only 20 miles southeast of downtown Tucson and is well worth the short journey, especially if you're traveling with children. It is located in the beautiful Rincon Mountains, a few miles south of the Saguaro National Park East, which offers spectacular desert views.

In 1992, The Colossal Cave Mountain Park expanded to an incredible 2,100 acres when it acquired La Posta Quemada Ranch near Vail. Many trails throughout this beautiful area, including the Arizona Trail, will soon be accessible to the public, and a museum is scheduled to open in the near future. For now, however, most of the park remains a working cattle ranch. Fortunately for Tucsonans who stay in town during the summer, the cool cave remains open year-round.

Colossal Cave is on the National Register of Historic Places, and is rich in legends that tour guides enthusiastically reveal. In 1879, the cave, which had been well known by Native Americans, was "discovered" by rancher Solomon Lick, and soon became a hideout for bandits who roamed the Southwest. The Southern Pacific Railroad ran through the nearby Pantano Wash, where two of the first six of the railroad company's train robberies occurred.

One of the more famous legends involves a train hold-up in 1887. Injured bandits fled into the cave, leaving dried blood stains at the entrance. They were later discovered in the town of Willcox boasting of their escape through a narrow shaft in the cave. Some even say that the bandits' stolen gold was left behind in this deep cavern, which still has not been entirely explored.

The roof of the limestone cave is bedecked with stalactites, deposits of calcite that drip into an icicle shaped formation. It also contains stalagmites – inverted stalactites that rise from the floor – and flowstone, which is calcite that has been deposited by flowing waters. The curved deposits of calcite that form as tiny water droplets emerge from their tips are called helictites. These natural formations have created such sights as "The Kingdom of the Elves," "The Frozen Waterfall," and "The Drapery Room."

The first cave tours were given in 1923 and required many ropes and powerful lanterns. Today, the 45-minute tour through Colossal Cave requires little in the way of safety equipment and special precautions. The convenient walkways and lighting system constructed in the cave by the Civilian Conservation Corps in the mid-1930s make it extremely accessible and safe, even for children. It's so easily accessible, in fact, that the cave served as the setting for the Walt Disney film, *The Outlaw Cats of Colossal Cave.*

Tours usually leave every 10 to 30 minutes throughout the day, and no special clothing is required. The cave remains at a cool 70°F all year and is always dry, thus preventing the formations from growing. This feature makes Colossal Cave unlike any cave in the country.

If your underground tour leaves your stomach feeling cavernous as well, vending machines and an outdoor hot dog stand are located on the premises. There is a nice picnic facility right outside the cave, for those who choose to relax on their own.

In addition to the standard cave tours, private parties may now reserve a hayride, cowboy cookout, or even a candlelight tour of the cave through Reddington Land & Cattle Company at Cascabel Ranch (520-721-9090). Camping is also available within a half mile of the cave entrance.

Address: P.O. Box 689, Oracle, AZ 85623; Highway 77, Mile Marker 96.5

Phone: 520-896-6200

Hours: Hours vary according to season; call for details.

Admission: Prices subject to change; call for current prices.

Chances are that you will have heard of Biosphere 2 even before coming to Tucson. This is the place where, on September 26, 1991, four men and four women entered into the world's first miniature biosphere, embarking on a two-year experiment that made international news.

Since that time, Biosphere 2 has undergone some major changes in scientific direction, and there are no current plans to send another team of scientists to live in the facility. Instead, a new research consortium from major universities and government agencies has come together and shifted the focus from human experimentation to research in the earth sciences.

Biosphere 2 is well adapted to accommodate visitors, but as you will be spending a lot of time outdoors, make sure to dress appropriately and wear lots of sunscreen. Allow a good three hours for the full experience. Tours leave about every hour of the day, and guides are knowledgeable and willing to entertain questions of all kinds.

Biosphere 2 is located north of Tucson at the foot of the Santa Catalina Mountains.

Tours begin at the Orientation Center. While waiting for the next available tour, there are various exhibits to see, including a large rotating model of Biosphere 2 to help give you an overall view of the site. The first phase of the tour is a 20-minute film in the Orientation Center that traces the development of Biosphere 2 and discusses the original goals and purposes of the project.

Courtesy of Biosphere 2

From there, a guide will lead you outside and down to the Analog Greenhouses, where you will get a more personal view of what it's like inside Biosphere 2. The greenhouses contain plants from tropical rain forests, deserts, savannas, and other ecosystems. Not far from these greenhouses is the Lab Exhibit, where many preliminary experiments were done in preparation for the implementation of Biosphere 2.

The final phase of the tour takes place outside the tall glass domes that encompass Biosphere 2. Miniature versions of a tropical rain forest, savanna, marsh, ocean, and agricultural farm are all visible outside the structure. The ocean in Biosphere 2 is the largest human-made ocean in the world, and its fish and other organisms can be seen underwater from the Ocean Viewing Gallery.

You'll also see the Biofair, a park full of hands-on scientific exhibits that are especially enjoyable for children. These exhibits include a giant kaleidoscope, a tornado simulator, and a human-size maze.

There are a few food options available near Biosphere 2. The Biosphere Café is located near the entrance. It offers a lovely perspective on the Catalina Mountains, and serves a breakfast buffet, lunch, and dinner. The Sphere Bookstore and Espresso Bar is located on your way to Biosphere 2. They serve baked goods and a fine cup of coffee. The Inn at the Biosphere offers accommodations with nice amenities and spectacular views.

International Wildlife Museum

Address: 4800 W. Gates Pass Rd.

Phone: 520-624-4024

Hours: Daily from 9 a.m. to 5 p.m. Open all holidays except Thanksgiving, Christmas, and New Year's Day.

Admission: Adults $5, senior citizens $3.75, children 6-12 $1.50, children 5 and under free.

The International Wildlife Museum is a non-profit facility that gives you a chance to see carefully preserved wild animals in realistically recreated natural settings. The exhibits at the Wildlife Museum convey the excitement of big game hunting, and also include interactive computers to help you learn more about conservation and zoology. And, in the Petting Menagerie exhibit, you'll find specimens that you can touch – such as the fearsome wild boar – in unnervingly lifelike poses.

The museum's restaurant offers buffalo burgers (and beef ones, too), sandwiches, fries, and other fast foods. In the gift shop you'll find many crafts imported from Africa and South America.

Arizona Historical Society Museum

Address: 949 E. Second St.

Phone: 520-628-5774

Hours: M-Sat 10 a.m. to 4 p.m., Sunday 12 to 4 p.m.

Admission: Free.

The Arizona Historical Society has created a unique museum that gives you an overview of Arizona's history through a series of interesting and informative exhibits. The mining exhibit – which includes an underground tunnel, an assay office, a miner's tent, and a blacksmith's shop – recreates all facets of this Arizona industry. In the Oxcart to Auto display, you can trace the various trends in transportation, and learn about the history of bicycles and bicycling in the state. The Off the Record exhibition is a collection of antique phonographs and music boxes; you'll be especially impressed by the 1899 Polyphon music box and 1905 Columbia gramophone.

The museum also features a display of bronzes by Frank Polk, Period Rooms decorated in authentic Arizona Territory style, and an extensive Navajo Weaving exhibit. Allow at least an hour here for a thorough tour, then stop into the Old Territorial Bookstore, which carries volumes on Arizona history, literature of the Southwest, and Western lore. The gift shop has even more treasures to offer: everything from Oaxacan wooden animal sculptures to scenic postcards.

Arizona State Museum

Address: The University of Arizona Campus

Phone: 520-621-6302

Hours: M-Sat 10 a.m. to 5 p.m., Sun 12 to 5 p.m.

Admission: Free.

To gain a better understanding of Arizona and the history of its indigenous peoples, the Arizona State Museum is a good place to start. More than 100 years of anthropological research went into the creation of the museum's exhibits, which are as diverse as the peoples who have been inhabiting the Southwest for many millennia. The focus here is on contemporary Native Americans and prehistoric cultures of the southwestern United States and northwestern Mexico.

In the South Museum, you can see what life was like in a fourteenth century Mogollon cliff dwelling, or see what anthropological evidence shows that dogs were kept as pets over 2,000 years ago. One of the more extensive exhibits here is the Hopi pottery display, which demonstrates every step of the pottery making process, and also explains how pottery can be used by anthropologists to gain a wide variety of information about a culture. Another exhibit in the South Museum takes you through the steps involved in an archeological dig, explaining why archeologists dig and what they hope to learn in the process. The South Museum also houses exhibits of indigenous plants, animals, and minerals.

The North Museum houses "Paths of Life," a multi-media wing devoted to the cultural anthropology of ten Native American groups. The focus is on each groups' origin, history, and present lifestyle. The exhibit is quite extensive, with video terminals, dioramas, and artifacts from Seri, Tarahumara, Yaqui, O'odham, Colorado River Yuman, Southern Paiute, Pai, Western Apache, Navajo, and Hopi cultures. You can follow a young Yaqui boy as he learns the deer dance, or see how the Seri who live on the Sea of Cortez use plants and animals from both the desert and the ocean. "Paths of Life" should not be missed; in fact, it's so impressive that we recommend spending at least an hour in this exhibit alone.

Pima Air and Space Museum

Address: 6000 E. Valencia Rd.

Phone: 520-574-9658

Hours: Daily 9 a.m. to 5 p.m.; no one admitted after 4 p.m.

Admission: Adults $6, military personnel and senior citizens $5, juniors 10-17 $3, children 9 and under free.

The Pima Air and Space Museum is a dream come true for those who are interested in flight. The museum has hundreds of acres of aircraft on display, four hangars full of exhibits, and an authentic WWII barracks.

"Conceived in the interest of preserving tangible ar-

artifacts of our aviation history for the recreational welfare and education of our present and future generations," the museum exhibits artifacts that are indeed tangible. As you enter, you'll pass under a gargantuan cargo helicopter that's the size of a 7-Eleven store.

The planes on display outside have stanchions nearby that provide relevant information, and with the free exhibit guide, you can get the lowdown on each as you wander through. Most of the 100 or so aircraft outside the hangars are approachable, so you can see landing gear three times your height and survey the conditions in the cockpit. This outdoor display extends beyond the walls of the museum. At Davis Monthan Air Force Base, which is just northeast of the museum, 3,000-plus aircraft are stored on the more than 3,000 acres that make up the Aircraft Maintenance and Regeneration Center. This vast "graveyard" has become a popular spot for filming scenes in movies and music videos.

In the hangars you'll find technical exhibits about the materials used for fuel, and not-so-technical exhibits displaying military uniforms. Hangar One's exhibits are concerned with the history of flight, Hangar Two houses the Arizona Aviation Hall of Fame and the Space Gallery, and Hangar Three is the home of famous WWII aircraft, including the B-24. The 390th Memorial Hangar contains the famous B-17 "Flying Fortress" and memorabilia from the 390th Bomb Group and Strategic Missile Wing.

Pima Air and Space Museum is the largest privately funded museum in the world. It has more than 180 aircraft on display and provides a comprehensive look at America's aviation history.

The Boeing B-29 Super Fortress.

Courtesy of Pima Air and Space Museum

Those with a keen interest in aircraft will want to spend at least three hours at the museum, maybe even all day. Others should plan to stay for an hour and a half to two hours. The gift shop has many educational toys related to flight along with t-shirts, cards, and books. Wearing sunscreen and hats is definitely recommended year round.

Titan Missile Museum

Directions: Take I-19 south to Green Valley; take exit 69 west 1/10th of a mile past La Canada to the entrance.

Phone: 520-791-2929 for reservations and information.

Hours: Daily 9 a.m. to 5 p.m., with the last tour starting at 4 p.m.

Admission: Adults $5, senior citizens and military personnel $4, juniors 10-17 $3, and children under 10 free.

The last remaining Titan missile.

Courtesy of Titan Missile Museum

By 1987, all Titan II missile complexes were taken off alert and dismantled, and all missiles were destroyed except for one that's located 25 minutes south of Tucson near Green Valley. Today, the compound is leased from the U.S. Air Force, and is home to the Titan Missile Museum.

For anyone with a fascination for aeronautics or military history, a trip out to the museum is worthwhile. Even if you aren't especially curious about nuclear warheads, it's interesting to visit just to see where a large chunk of the tax dollars paid during the Cold War have landed.

The launch control center, where the equipment that could have eventually incited nuclear Armageddon is housed, is perhaps the most interesting part of the museum. The tour guides perform demonstrations of monitoring and count-down procedures. The actual Titan II missile is still located in the 146-foot-deep silo, and you're welcome to photograph it.

Outside the compound, you can see the gigantic 430,000-pound thrust engine that was once capable of propelling the missile 250,000 feet high in less than three minutes. There is also a gift shop that sells souvenir t-shirts and educational toys.

Kitt Peak

Directions: Take I-10 to I-19 and go south. Exit on Ajo Way and go west on Ajo (Hwy. 86) for about 35 miles to Kitt Peak Rd. (Hwy. 386). Turn left and follow this road for another 13 miles.

Phone: 520-318-8600; Public Information Office of NOAO in Tucson at 520-318-8204.

Hours: Daily from 9 a.m. to 3:45 p.m.; Closed Thanksgiving, Christmas Eve, Christmas Day, and New Year's Day.

The clear, blue skies, remoteness, and high altitude of Kitt Peak have made it one of the premier astronomy centers in the world. Just 56 miles southwest of Tucson, in the beautiful Quinlan Mountains of the Tohono O'odham Nation, Kitt Peak is home to dozens of telescopes. The giant white domes which house the telescopes sit at an elevation of 6,882 feet, along dramatic mountain ridges that offer a spectacular view.

There are more astronomy observatories within a 50-mile radius of Tucson than you'll find in any other area of comparable size in the world.

The National Optical Astronomy Observatories (NOAO), which has leased the 2,400 acres of Kitt Peak, is operated by the Association of Universities for Research in Astronomy (AURA), Inc. AURA is a not-for-profit corporation with a membership of 22 universities nationwide. NOAO houses two of its branches at the site: the Kitt Peak National Observatory and the National Solar Observatory. The National Observatory includes 4-meter and 2.1-meter telescopes that are both open to the public, and the National Solar Observatory contains the world's three largest solar telescopes.

All other telescopes are scheduled for use by astronomers every day or night of the year. Precious observing time is awarded to visiting and staff astronomers twice a year for the nighttime telescopes, and quarterly for the solar telescopes.

The 4-meter Mayall optical telescope that's open for public viewing has enormous light-gathering power. It is used mainly to view distant galaxies and quasars, and is housed in an 18-story building that's topped with a large white dome. The structure contains a glass-enclosed observation deck from which the entire observatory, and 100 miles of surrounding desert and mountains, can be viewed. On most days, even the mountain ranges of Mexico are visible.

A telescope that's available for public use is the Burrell-Schmidt telescope. This instrument is ideal for the observation of extended objects, such as globular clusters and nebulae.

A second telescope you may use is the 2.1-meter telescope of the National Observatory. The telescope building is surrounded by two towers that contain Coudé feed mirrors. These mirrors reflect light onto a polar axis to come to a focus at a fixed point, bringing the distant image into the range of vision.

The Visitors Center and museum on Kitt Peak have both undergone recent renovations. The exhibits explain many aspects of astronomy, and detail the research programs that are being conducted at the site. A new theater is also being constructed here. Informational films are shown throughout the day in the existing theater, and guided tours are held Monday through Friday at 11 a.m., 1 p.m., and 2:30 p.m., with an additional tour at 9:30 a.m. on weekends. If your visit doesn't coincide with the scheduled tours, the Visitors Center provides a very helpful self-tour brochure.

In addition to the astronomical attraction it provides, Kitt Peak is a naturally beautiful area that can offer a cool respite from the hot desert summer. In the winter, Kitt Peak is often one of the few areas around Tucson to have a snow cover. On the site, there is a picnic area with grills for those who wish to enjoy the outdoor air. There are no food facilities except for a soda and candy machine, so packing a lunch is key.

Mayall Telescope at Kitt Peak.

Courtesy of National Optical Astronomy Observatories

While driving up the mountain road that leads to the site, you may see a few cyclists testing their endurance. Hiking in the area requires a permit from the Tohono O'odham Nation. The best time of year to see wildflowers on your way to Kitt Peak is from late March to early June. You can expect to see purple lupine and sunny poppies. The ocotillo, prickly pear, and saguaro cacti that line the road after the Kitt Peak turnoff are likely to be blooming in May or June.

*Address: The University of Arizona Campus
(E. University Blvd. and N. Cherry Ave.)*

*Phone: Special events and workshops 520-621-4515;
laser light shows 520-621-7827.*

*Hours: M-F 9 a.m. to 5 p.m., Sat-Sun 1 to 5 p.m.,
Wed-Th 7 to 9 p.m., F-Sat 7 p.m. to midnight.*

*Admission: $2 for non-theatergoers (up to 4 children under 13
free with paying adult), $3-$5 for theater viewings.*

Flandrau Science Center is conveniently located on the University of Arizona's campus, within walking distance of several other campus museums and galleries. Most of the exhibits are "hands-on," which makes the Center a fun and interesting place for kids of all ages. The comprehensive section of spatial reasoning puzzles and games is both challenging and instructional. One exhibit, "Colliding Asteroids," explains the nature of asteroids and allows you to examine real meteorite samples that have been collected from all over the world. There are also many exhibits related to optics, an extensive mineral museum, and a gift shop that sells

Courtesy of UofA Flandrau Science Center

Flandrau Science Center located on the University of Arizona campus.

science-related toys and books. Allow an hour or more to visit the Science Center.

You can also enjoy several types of evening events at Flandrau. The shows are quite spectacular and diverse. One night you can see a Nirvana and Pearl Jam laser light display and the next listen to Baxter Black the Cowboy Astronomer's unique stories and humor about the heavenly bodies. The admission price for shows varies, but it's never more than $6.

Depending on the weather, which is usually conducive to star-gazing, the Center's telescope is available for the public Tuesday through Saturday from 8:30 to 10:30 p.m. Call the number above for information on the scheduling and prices of shows and telescope availability.

Center for Creative Photography

Address: The University of Arizona Campus

Phone: 520-621-7968

Hours: M-F 11 a.m. to 5 p.m., Closed Saturday, Sunday 12 to 5 p.m.

Admission: Free.

Shell, *1927* *photo by* *Edward Weston.*

The world-renowned Center for Creative Photography is a must-see for photography buffs and anyone interested in the arts. The center includes galleries with ever-changing exhibits, photographers' archives, a library, and more than 50,000 photographs. Richard Avedon, Paul Strand, Ansel Adams, Marion Palfi, Edward Weston, and over 1,400 other photographers all have representative work at the center. Call the center for information on current exhibits.

A unique aspect of the center is its print viewing facility. You are welcome to use the print viewing room to examine photos from the extensive photographers' archives or from the photograph collection during specified hours. Reservations for use of this facility are highly recommended, so be sure to call ahead to ensure its availability.

The gift shop is a great place to find interesting books and unusual cards.

University of Arizona Museum of Art

Address: The University of Arizona Campus

Phone: 520-621-7567

Hours: M-F 9 a.m. to 5 p.m., Sunday 12 to 4 p.m.
Summer hours (May 15-Labor Day) M-F 10 a.m. to 3:30 p.m., Sunday 12 to 4 p.m. Closed Saturday and University holidays.

Admission: Free.

Located right on campus, the University of Arizona Museum of Art is within easy walking distance of the University's other museums and the Student Union. Its permanent collection of more than 4,000 pieces includes works by O'Keefe, Rembrandt, and Picasso. Exhibits are rotated, so if there is something special you'd like to see that is not on display, you can arrange a private viewing with museum curators. The UAMA also houses 26 panels from the fifteenth century Spanish altarpiece of the Cathedral of Ciudad Rodrigo, and more contemporary works like Audrey Flack's "Marilyn."

One of the most interesting and comprehensive exhibits is that of sculptor Jacques Lipchitz. The collection of 61 plaster and clay models, a gift from the artist's widow, gives you the opportunity to see the complete process of sculpting, as many of the pieces are unfinished works inspired by fleeting creative impulses.

Docents are available on the first and last Wednesday of each month for tours through the 14,000 square feet of exhibition space. The informative tours begin at 12:15 p.m. The museum offers special tours, lunch-time discussions and workshops, performances, and lectures each month. Call for details.

The bookstore stocks a variety of books, cards, catalogs and posters. It is open during the same hours as the museum.

Tucson Museum of Art

Address: 140 N. Main Ave.

Phone: 520-624-2333

Hours: M-Sat 10 a.m. to 4 p.m., Sunday 12 to 4 p.m.

Admission: Adults $2, students with current ID $1, children under 12 free.

Located in the heart of downtown, the Tucson Museum of Art is more than just gallery space; it's a year-round center for concerts, art festivals, and classes. A major part of the museum is the Historic Block, five well-preserved buildings that date back to the 1800s.

Like any city's art museum, the Tucson Museum of Art hosts several exhibitions each year. Recently it was the

The Night-Riders *by Olaf Wieghorst.*

home to a multicultural collection of shoebox sculptures – pieces small enough to fit in a shoebox – and an exhibit of giant paintings from the museum's permanent collection.

Docent-led tours may be scheduled by calling 520-624-2333. The knowledgeable docents can answer questions and provide a wealth of information about the Historic Block.

The gift shop carries hand-crafted works by local artists, as well as cards and prints. It keeps the same hours as the museum, and has something for everyone.

Refer to El Presido map on page 16.

Tucson Children's Museum

Address: 200 S. 6th Ave.
Phone: 520-884-7511
Hours: Tu-Fri 9 a.m. to 1 p.m., Saturday 10 a.m. to 5 p.m., Sunday 1 to 5 p.m.
Admission: Adults $3.00, senior citizens $1.50, children $1.50

Having fun with face painting at the Tucson Children's Museum.

If you're looking for a good place to visit with your children, especially those between the ages of 3 and 12, the Tucson Children's Museum is where you'll want to start. Located in a downtown historical district, the museum has many exhibits that cater to a child's natural desire to touch and play with everything. From experimenting with magnets to blowing bubbles to creating an image in the shadow room, children feel both intrigued and excited as they roam throughout the museum.

Courtesy of Tucson Children's Museum

The museum is divided into several rooms, each of which emphasizes a particular area of interest, such as machinery, science, natural history, energy, and the two most popular for many children: the firehouse and costume area. While there is a learning element to many of the exhibits, having fun is the primary goal, and most of the displays are designed accordingly. Parents of children 5 and under will appreciate The Kidspace, a special room filled with big, colorful toys that are designed to keep the younger ones occupied while older brothers or sisters explore from room to room.

Refer to Armory Park map on page 21.

Tucson Botanical Gardens

Address: 2150 N. Alvernon Way

Phone: 520-326-9255

*Hours: Gardens – daily 8:30 a.m. to 4:30 p.m.; Gift shop –
M-Sat 9 a.m. to 4 p.m., Sunday 12 to 4 p.m.*

*Admission: Suggested donation: Adults $3, senior citizens $2,
children free of charge.*

Have you ever wondered what a vanilla plant or coffee tree looks like? Which plants best attract birds? How to landscape a desert yard? At Tucson Botanical Gardens, you can find the answers to these questions and countless others. During your tour, you'll enjoy much more than the pretty flowers and sculptured shrubbery that are standard fare at most botanical gardens. The Tucson Botanical Gardens is home to hundreds of exotic plants that can thrive in southern Arizona, and the variety of plant life on the grounds and the classes offered make it a valuable educational resource.

Originally the residence of the Porter family, the construction of the buildings and various gardens commenced in the 1920s. Development continued until 1968, when the property was donated and converted into the Tucson Botanical Gardens.

Upon your arrival, you may request a useful and complete brochure to take a self-guided tour of the grounds. During your walk, you'll encounter at least a dozen dramatically different gardens and fascinating displays. One of the first that you are likely to enter is the charming Historical Garden, which includes olive trees, lilacs and English ivy, all of which were planted in the early 1900s. There are also examples of the Mediterranean varieties of shrubs and trees that were popular in Tucson in the early part of the century.

Another beautiful garden is the Xeriscape Garden, a lush and colorful garden that requires a surprisingly small amount of water and care. There is also the blooming Wildflower Garden, where Mexican Gold Poppies, desert marigolds, blue lupines, red penstemons, and others flaunt their colors. The time to catch these flowers in action is during the months of March, April, and May.

You mustn't leave Tucson Botanical Gardens without visiting The Tropical Greenhouse. Within this little greenhouse reside coffee plants, banana trees, vanilla plants, and fern varieties. Be sure to smell their many aromas. Children especially appreciate learning where their vanilla ice cream gets its flavor.

Tucson Botanical Gardens also has a very extensive Herb Garden. The herbal history of the Southwest is unique, largely because of the missionaries and settlers who came here from many parts of the world. They couldn't leave their favorite herbs behind, and luckily this arid region proved to be a hospitable place in which to grow them. The extremely large variety of herbs that can be grown in Tucson is thoroughly represented and clearly marked in this garden, and hopefully you will walk away with a new idea or two for your own herb collection.

There are many varieties of cacti within the desert landscape, including the magnificent saguaros that are indigenous only to the Sonoran Desert.

Native varieties of cacti and succulents share their turf with imports from around the world in the Rodney Engard Cactus and Succulent Garden. You should also make your way to the Native Seeds SEARCH garden which includes Hopi string beans, Tohono O'odham corn, and other Native American crops. Native American gardening techniques are also on display.

In addition to its spectacular gardens, Tucson Botanical Gardens has many other exhibits to offer. There is a Tohono O'odham Round House on the premises – an amazing structure that is constructed entirely of Sonoran Desert plant materials. Another interesting display is the Tucson Organic Gardening Club Compost Demonstration Site. There are several different ways to maintain a successful backyard composting system. If you have never tried composting at home, and you want to avoid the risk of trial and error, this site can provide many ideas on how to develop an effective composting program.

Learning opportunities abound in the garden. The education program offers classes and workshops, including gardening for the Tucson newcomer, ethnobotany, herbal remedies, irrigation, and summer activities for children. Other events include spring and fall plant sales, a Home Garden Tour, summer Herb Fair, the fall Chile Fiesta, and Holiday Luminaria Night. Guided tours are available on Wednesdays, Saturdays, and Sundays at 10 a.m., but since schedules are subject to change, it's a good idea to call ahead.

Old Pueblo Trolley

Phone: 520-792-1802

Hours: *Friday 6 p.m. to 12 a.m., Saturday 10 a.m. to 12 a.m., and Sunday 12 p.m. to 6 p.m.*

Fares: *One-way fares – $1 for adults and 50¢ children 6-12; All-day fares – $2.50 for adults and $1.25 for children 6-12.*

The Old Pueblo Trolley.

Ed Armstrong

If your feet tire easily, or if you don't feel like walking from one end of Fourth Avenue Shopping District to the other, you'll enjoy this great weekend attraction: Old Pueblo Trolley's electric street car. The trolley line starts at North Fourth Avenue and East 8th Street and continues north to University Avenue, where it turns east and heads to University Square. After your shopping, sightseeing and trolley ride, if you're ready to shop some more, the Campbell Avenue shopping area is just a short ride by car to the north.

To help you make the most of your time in Tucson, we've compiled the following maps of area attractions that are within close proximity of one another in and outside of downtown. Several of the sights in the Attractions section lie outside the areas described below, but are well-worth the special trip.

University Area

❶ *Old Pueblo Trolley*

❷ *Arizona Historical Society Museum*

❸ *Arizona State Museum*

❹ *University of Arizona Museum of Art*

❺ *Center for Creative Photography*

❻ *Flandrau Science Center*

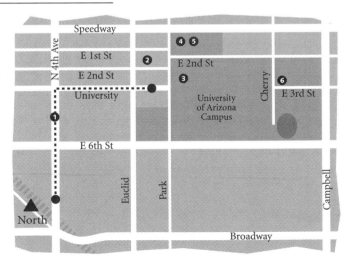

West of Tucson

1 *Arizona-Sonora Desert Museum*

2 *International Wildlife Museum*

3 *Old Tucson Studios*

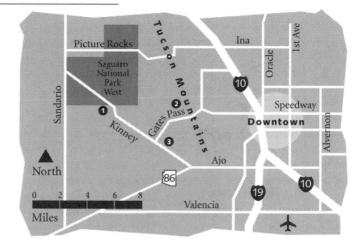

North of Tucson

1 *De Grazia's Gallery in the Sun*

2 *Sabino Canyon*

3 *Tohono Chul Park*

4 *Biosphere 2*

5 *Tucson Botanical Gardens*

6 *Reid Park Zoo*

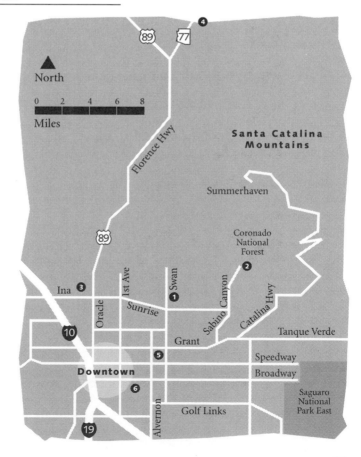

Tucson has some of the best restaurants in the nation, with a great variety of cuisine that includes Mexico City and Sonoran-style Mexican, sublime Southwestern-style fare, innovative Italian, fresh fast foods, and more. The area's offerings also cover a broad scale of atmospheres and prices – from authentic hole-in-the-wall burrito places and casual coffee houses, to contemporary culinary venues and the more formal and sometimes spendy dining experiences. This list is by no means exhaustive, but we think it includes some of the best places to dine in Tucson.

El Saguarito

Address: 7216 N. Oracle Rd.

Phone: 520-297-1264

Hours: Mon-Sat 7 a.m. to 9 p.m.; Closed Sunday.

Remarks: $, NS, CC, RS, Beer and Wine, P

Restaurant Remark Guide

$ *Under $10*

$$ *Between $10-$20*

$$$ *Between $20-$40*

$$$$ *Above $40*

S *Smoking*

NS *Non Smoking*

RS *Reservations Accepted*

CH *Checks*

CC *Credit Cards Accepted*

FB *Full Bar*

P *Patio*

The price ratings indicate the average cost of a complete meal for one person, and does not include the cost of alcoholic drinks, taxes or tips.

El Saguarito was one of the first Mexican restaurants in Arizona to use canola oil, and prides itself on using heart-healthy ingredients. The vegetarian burro at this family-oriented restaurant is very unique, full of squash and other veggies, and we love the sweet, spicy chicken mole, fiery salsa, and flavorful, fresh guacamole. El Saguarito's owner, Albert Vasquez, has recently introduced a new menu called *El Corazon Contento* ("the happy heart"), on which all dishes fall under the 20% fat-to-calorie ratio recommended by the American Heart Association. Vasquez has also added lower fat baked tortilla chips to his current menu.

El Minuto

Address: 354 S. Main Ave.

Phone: 520-882-4145

Hours: Sun-Th 11 a.m. to 11 p.m., F-Sat 11 a.m. to 2 a.m.

Remarks: $$, S, NS, CC, CH, RS, FB

The food at El Minuto is delicious, especially the chicken enchiladas with red sauce and the tortilla soup. The hospitality is always warm and friendly even on the busiest of evenings. Located in the Barrio Historico, right next to El Tiradito, "The Wishing Shrine" (see the listing in the Historic District section for more information), this is a great place to take visitors. The Barrio is well worth exploring, as it has many expressive murals and brightly colored homes.

El Charro

Address: 311 N. Court Ave.

Phone: 520-622-1922

Hours: Sun-Th 11 a.m. to 9 p.m., F-Sat 11 a.m. to 10 p.m.

Remarks: $$, Smoking on Patio Only, CC, CH, RS, FB, P

El Charro boasts of serving "Tucson-style" and traditional

Courtesy of El Charro

The intimate patio of ¡Toma!.

central Mexican cuisine. Known for their *carne seca*, they also have giant quesadillas, chimichangas, and a large selection of moles. Attached to the restaurant is ¡Toma!, a full and festive bar complete with good Mexican beers, and a charming gift shop that carries a variety of Tucson-style treats. It is located in the El Presidio Historic District in a stone-accented building which dates back to the 1880s.

Mi Nidito

Address: 1813 S. 4th Ave.

Phone: 520-622-5081

Hours: Sun, W-Th 11 a.m. to 10:30 p.m., F-Sat 11 a.m. to 2 a.m.

Remarks: $$, S, NS, CC, CH, Beer and Wine

Usually there is a long line at this restaurant, but the food you'll enjoy here is well worth the wait. This is a true Tucson institution – it's been in business in the same location for more than 40 years. Fresh, delicious, and authentic dishes are prepared by native chefs, and menudo is served daily along with delicious topopos, chimichangas, and flautas. The margaritas here are also very good.

La Placita Café

Address: Plaza Palomino, 2950 N. Swan Rd.

Phone: 520-881-1150

Hours: M-Sat 11 a.m. to 9 p.m., M-Sun 5 p.m. to 9 p.m.

Remarks: $$, S, NS, CC, CH, RS, FB, P

Delicious food and gracious service make La Placita an excellent choice. The restaurant is small and elegant, and offers a wide array of flavorful Sonoran dishes. Tasty dinner options include the Fresh Cabrilla Fish with tomatoes, onions, and chilies, and the well-loved Chiles Rellenos de Cangrejo, stuffed with succulent crab meat.

La Fuente

Address: 1749 N. Oracle Rd.

Phone: 520-623-8659

Hours: Sun-Th 11:30 a.m. to 10 p.m., F-Sat 11:30 a.m. to 11 p.m.

Remarks: $$, S, NS, CC, CH, RS, FB

Run by the same family for 35 years, this is a beautiful place to take visitors for a meal. Mariachi music is a nightly event, except on Mondays. La Fuente serves authentic Sonoran-style Mexican food and is known for its *mole poblano de gallina.* If you've never had it, you must try the mole sauce, which contains the odd, yet delicious combination of unsweetened chocolate, chilies, and spices. The restaurant also offers some good vegetarian options.

Southwestern and Innovative Cuisine

Blue Willow

Address: 2616 N. Campbell Ave.

Phone: 520-795-8736

Hours: M-F 7 a.m. to 10 p.m., Sat-Sun 7 a.m. to 11 p.m.

Remarks: $, S, NS, CC, CH, RS, Beer and Wine, P

With over two dozen combinations, the Blue Willow offers the best selection of omelets in town! The portions are huge and remain available throughout lunch and dinner. Many vegetarian choices are available, including delicious and unusual salads. Set in a restored house, the restaurant has a great gift shop that carries one of the best inventories of greeting cards in Tucson. A walled-in patio, filled with tall foliage and complete with heaters for chilly evenings, makes outdoor dining pleasurable year-round.

Café Magritte

Address: 254 E. Congress St.

Phone: 520-884-8004

Hours: Sun, Tu-Th 11 a.m. to 11 p.m., F-Sat 11 a.m. to 12 a.m.

Remarks: $$, S, NS, CC, CH, RS, Beer and Wine, P

The sandwiches, soups, salads, and other dishes you'll find here are perhaps some of the most creative in the city. Asian, Southwestern, and Mediterranean tastes are all present. Desserts are also irresistible. The dining areas are comfortable and artistic and you can sit outside and watch the happenings on Congress Street.

Trio Bistro and Bar

Address: *Plaza Palomino, 2990 N. Swan Rd.*

Phone: *520-325-3333*

Hours: *M-Th 11:30 a.m. to 10 p.m., F-Sat 11 p.m. to 11 p.m.*

Remarks: *$$, S, NS, CC, CH, RS, FB, P*

Trio Bistro and Bar offers an excellent selection of dishes that reflect Latin American, Southeast Asian, and Mediterranean influences. Quality and variety are excellent – everyone at the table can enjoy something totally different. The barbecued trout is scrumptious, and soups, including the lemon-grass, are lovely. The Moroccan vegetables are spicy, delicious, and served over a fluffy plate of cous-cous. The decor is equally cross-cultural, with aluminum siding walls and huge rolling doors that can close off various dining areas. Desserts are also exotic; finishing your meal with some delectable crêpes is a must.

Café Poca Cosa

Address: *88 E. Broadway Ave. and 20 N. Scott Ave.*

Phone: *E. Broadway Ave. – 520-622-6400,*
N. Scott Ave. – 520-622-6400

Hours: *M-Th 11 a.m. to 9 p.m., F-Sat 11 a.m. to 10 p.m.*

Remarks: *$$, Smoking in Bar and Patio only, CC, CH, RS, FB, P*

You can be sure that whatever you order at either location of Café Poca Cosa will be delicious, exciting, and out of the ordinary. The menu changes daily, and often incorporates tropical fruits, beans, chicken, and even chocolate. Entree choices may include such dishes as Pollo en Salsa Casera (shredded chicken dressed with mild chiles and tomatoes), or the unusual and popular shredded beef and scrambled egg dish, *machaca,* which is seasoned with delicate spices. We also love the piquant red snapper that's served with tomatoes and onions. The colorful patio at the larger Broadway site is a great place to dine on pleasant afternoons and evenings.

Café Terra Cotta

Address: *St. Philip's Plaza, 4310 N. Campbell Ave.*

Phone: *520-577-8100*

Hours: *Sun-Th 11 a.m. to 9:30 p.m. F-Sat 11 a.m. to 11 p.m.*

Remarks: *$$$, Smoking on Patio Only, CC, CH, RS, FB, P*

Café Terra Cotta is tastefully decorated with a Southwestern theme. The menu is organized by Starters, Small Plates, Salads, Appetite Whetters, Soups, Sandwiches, Entrees, Pizza, and Desserts. You may find it unnecessary to order entrees because the rest of the menu is so extensive, and there are also some very tasty vegetarian choices. Entrees may include the spicy seafood specialty known as "eskalar," which is a white fish rubbed with ground red chile, then grilled "scorpion style," and covered with a dressing of guajillo peppers and fresh oranges. Shrimp flautas come on the side. The desserts are on display and hard to refuse – especially the crème brulée – so save room.

Boccata

Address: River Center, 5605 E. River Rd.
Phone: 520-577-9309
Hours: Sun-Th 5:30 p.m. to 9 p.m., F-Sat 5 p.m. to 10 p.m.
Remarks: $$$, S, NS, CC, CH, RS, FB, P

Here you can sample a wide range of cuisines that include Northern Italian, Southern French, new American, and Cuban. Boccata's menu changes seasonally, with rotating regional and daily menus. Mussels in white wine and garlic are highly praised, and the bouillabaisse is extraordinary. For a spectacular view of the Tucson valley, ask for a seat on the restaurant's lovely terrace.

Ovens Restaurant

Address: St. Philip's Plaza, 4820 N. Campbell Ave.
Phone: 520-577-9001
Hours: Sun-Th 11 a.m. to 9:30 p.m., F-Sat 11 a.m. to 10 p.m.
Remarks: $$$, S, NS, CC, CH, RS, FB, P

The open kitchen at Ovens features a wood-burning oven that cooks up delicious pizza with such gourmet toppings as sundried tomatoes and goat cheese. A combination "pizza salad" is full of fresh baby greens, and another great possibility is the Chinese Chicken Salad. Desserts are just as delicious and creative. Dining rooms are spacious and light, and the patio extremely pleasant.

Janos

Address: *150 N. Main Ave.*

Phone: *520-884-9426*

Hours: *(Mid May through Nov.) Tu-Sat 5:30 p.m. to closing; (Dec. to Mid May) M-Sat 5:30 p.m. to closing*

Remarks: *$$$$, Smoking on Patio Only, CC, CH, RS, FB, P*

Travel and Leisure has called him "one of the finest cooks in America," and once you experience a meal by Chef Janos Wilder, you will understand why. Janos experimented with French and Southwestern tastes for more than a year before opening Tucson's most fascinating restaurant, and the cuisine you'll find here is like no other place in the world. Since then the restaurant has won several major culinary awards, including the Fine Dining Award as one of the top eight Contemporary Restaurants in the nation, and The Mobil Travel Guide has given it the Four Star Award.

Courtesy of Janos

Not only is the food outstanding at Janos, but the restaurant is located in the historic landmark of the Hiram Stevens House, an adobe dating back to 1856. This extremely charming space is filled with separate dining rooms, each of which has a distinct charm. The service at Janos is professional and very warm. In fact, if you request a tour of the home, the staff will be happy to accommodate you.

Chef Janos Wilder in his renowned restaurant.

An exciting, new Janos-offshoot that's open for lunch is Wild Johnny's Wagon. Hitched up just behind the restaurant in the Tucson Museum of Art Plaza, this contemporary walk-up lunch stand recalls the feeling of the chuckwagons of old. Here, you can graze along the Buckboard Buffet Anti-Pasta bar, or enjoy the substantial Vegetarian Dagwood, a mountainous sandwich that's stuffed with fresh ingredients grown by local farmers. Shaded tables offer a perfect place to linger over lunch and steal some respite from the sun. Whatever you choose, you can be sure that your luncheon selection will bear the mark of quality and innovation that has made Janos one of Tucson's premier dining locations.

L'il Abner's Steakhouse

Address: 8501 N. Silverbell Rd.
Phone: 520-744-2800
Hours: Sun-Th 5 p.m. to 10 p.m., F-Sat 5 p.m. to 11 p.m.
Remarks: $$, S, NS, CC, RS, P

L'il Abner's Steakhouse has long perpetuated the Tucson tradition of serving up delicious ribs, chicken, and of course, steak. Flavorful steaks come in different sizes – from large to huge – and are grilled over mesquite to perfection. The exceptional cuisine is augmented by live music on the weekends, with Dean Armstrong and the Arizona Dance Hands whipping up the Western music on Friday and Saturday nights, and the Titan Valley Warheads twanging out great bluegrass on Sunday evenings.

Pinnacle Peak

Address: 6541 E. Tanque Verde Rd.
Phone: 520-296-0911
Hours: M-Sun 5 p.m. to 10 p.m.
Remarks: $$, S, NS, CC, CH, FB

"Home of the Famous Cowboy Steak," Pinnacle Peak is located in the animated Trail Dust Town. The authentic saloon, mesquite grill, and the Savoy Opera House make this a true Western experience. While you soak in the atmosphere, you can feast on cowboy grub, including steaks cut only from the short loin – the true cowboy's choice.

Pinnacle Peak restaurant in Trail Dust Town.

Ed Armstrong

El Corral

Address: 2201 E. River Rd.	

Address: 2201 E. River Rd.

Phone: 520-299-6092

Hours: M-Fri 5 p.m. to 10 p.m., Sat-Sun 4:30 p.m. to 10 p.m.

Remarks: $$, S, NS, CC, CH, FB

Located in charming old adobe ranch house, El Corral is a popular spot to enjoy a Western meal. The prime rib is excellent, or try other beef cuts, chicken entrees, or the popular tamale pie. The Chocolate Mudpie Dessert is a must-eat, so be sure to save some room.

Grills

Dakota Café and Catering Company

Address: 6541 E. Tanque Verde Rd. (Trail Dust Town)

Phone: 520-298-7188

Hours: M-Th 11:30 a.m. to 3 p.m. and 5 p.m. to 10 p.m., F-Sat 11 a.m. to 10 p.m., closed Sunday.

Remarks: $$, S, NS, CC, CH, RS, FB, P

Located in Trail Dust Town, Dakota Café is a contemporary restaurant that's set in a lively nineteenth century Western town environment. The cafe features fresh fish daily and many vegetarian choices, including such specialties as tempura coconut shrimp with chutney marmalade. The salads are huge, and the atmosphere is casual. There's even a pleasant patio. Most of the original art that hangs on the walls is available for purchase.

Kingfisher

Address: 2564 E. Grant Rd.

Phone: 520-323-7739

Hours: M-F 11 a.m. to 12 a.m., Sat-Sun 5 p.m. to 12 a.m.

Remarks: $$$, S, NS, CC, CH, RS

The Kingfisher has an ever-changing menu with an extensive oyster bar. The decor is modern and open, and the service is excellent and personal. A comprehensive light menu is also available. Entrees may include such specialties as

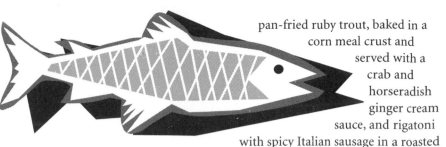

pan-fried ruby trout, baked in a corn meal crust and served with a crab and horseradish ginger cream sauce, and rigatoni with spicy Italian sausage in a roasted pepper cream sauce is another favorite. It can be crowded here, so we recommend making a reservation.

Buddy's Grill

Address: 4821 E. Grant Rd.

Phone: 520-95-2226

Hours: Sun-Th 11 a.m. to 10:30 p.m., F-Sat 11 a.m. to 11 p.m.

Remarks: $$, S, NS, CC, CH, RS, FB

Offering a fine selection for almost any taste, Buddy's cooks up everything from seafood, steaks, and salads to satisfying sandwiches and juicy hamburgers. Despite the challenges of offering such a diverse menu, the chefs at Buddy's carefully maintain quality and excellent flavor in every dish. The service is first-rate, too.

Presidio Grill

Address: 3352 E. Speedway Blvd.

Phone: 520-327-4667

Hours: M-Th 11 a.m. to 10 p.m., F-Sat 11 a.m. to 12 a.m., Sun 8 a.m. to 10 p.m.

Remarks: $$$, S, NS, CC, RS, FB

The excellent food at the Presidio Grill is borderline Southwest, and the chef uses a lot of Poblano chilies and garlic. The atmosphere is modern – with marble, steel, and wood decor – and the service is excellent. In addition to the outstanding fare you'll enjoy at this contemporary grill, there is often live entertainment in the evenings, which might include flamenco dance, and blues or jazz music. The restaurant also hosts special supper club events that center on specific themes; call for details and schedules.

Keaton's

Address: Foothills Mall, 7401 N. La Cholla Blvd., and
6464 E. Tanque Verde Rd.

Phone: Foothills Mall – 520-297-1999,
E. Tanque Verde – 520-721-1299

Hours: M-Sat 11:30 a.m. to 10 p.m., Sun 10:30 a.m. to 10 p.m.

Remarks: $$$, S, NS, CC, CH, RS, FB, P

The oyster bar at Keaton's is plentiful and delicious – just like the rest of the menu. Offerings include seafood, big burgers and other grilled meats, salads, and specialty dishes. Grilled New York Sirloin is a pleaser. It's served with a peppery and charred-tasting seasoning that perfectly complements the accompanying Bordelaise sauce. The scallopini are hard to beat – the fresh basil and white wine sauce is delicious.

City Grill

Address: 6350 E. Tanque Verde Rd.

Phone: 520-733-1111

Hours: M-Sat 11 a.m. to 10 p.m., Sun 11 a.m. to 9 p.m.

Remarks: $$, S, NS, CC, CH, RS, FB, P

City Grill specializes in innovative American cuisine served in an atmosphere that's at once upscale and casual. Colorful murals and fine art – most of the movable pieces are for sale – cover the walls of the chic main dining room. Cozy booths and a few contemporary tables sit under the spacious restaurant's high ceiling. Gourmet pizzas baked in a wood-fired oven, fresh grilled seafood, flavorful pasta dishes, and uniquely dressed rotisserie chicken are among the most popular options. Choose from the restaurant's extensive wine list, then take your glass over to the Exhibition Kitchen to watch the chefs at work.

Anthony's in the Catalinas

Address: 6440 N. Campbell Ave.

Phone: 520-299-1771

Hours: M-Sat 11:30 a.m. to 2:30 p.m., M-Sun 5:30 p.m. to 10 p.m.

Remarks: $$$, S, NS, CC, CH, RS, FB, P

A visit to Anthony's is a truly elegant experience; the restaurant has the best view of the Tucson valley and surrounding mountains. Along with its impressive perspective and absolutely impeccable service, Anthony's has the most extensive wine list in Arizona. There are more than 1,600 choices, ranging in price from $30 to nearly $2,000.

The moment you sit down, you'll be served a sampling of some of the exquisite food to come: a complimentary plate of lahvosh with salmon mousse. An excellent variety of appetizers is available, along with several hot and cold soups and salads. 26 entrees make deciding what to eat even more difficult. Many rave about the lamb Wellington with mushroom duxelle under flaky pastry. Southwestern influence has helped to create such dishes as steak au poivre flambé with green peppercorn sauce. For vegetarians, spinach tortellini is a tantalizing option. Desserts are extraordinary, especially the Bananas Foster à deux that's prepared tableside.

The Arizona Inn

Address: 2200 East Elm St.

Phone: 520-325-1541

Hours: M-Sun 7 a.m. to 10:30 a.m., 11:30 a.m. to 2 p.m., 5 p.m. to 10 p.m., Sunday Brunch 11 a.m. to 2 p.m.

Remarks: $$$, S, NS, CC, CH, RS, FB, P

For a historic, charming, and elegant experience, head straight to The Arizona Inn. The oldest resort hotel in Tucson, the Inn has been in operation since the 1930s, and is a wonderful place to go for breakfast, lunch, or a formal dinner. There are several informal dining rooms and one formal dining room that has high beamed ceilings and attractive table settings.

The menu here changes seasonally. Examples of delectable appetizers include herbed cheese terrine, and Greek-style stuffed grape leaves with dill yogurt sauce. Entrees include several game selections, such as smoked quail with pecan-apple stuffing. Tournedos of beef are broiled and served with a biting pistachio mole. The service is professional, attentive, and friendly. There is a prix fixe menu available which includes soup or salad, entrée, and dessert.

The Tack Room

Address: 2800 N. Sabino Canyon Rd.
Phone: 520-722-2800
Hours: Daily from 6 p.m. to 9:30 p.m.; closed on Mondays during the summer.
Remarks: $$$$, S, NS, CC, RS, FB

One of only two five-star restaurants west of St. Louis, the Tack Room has been one of Tucson's most refined restaurants for more than three decades. Though atmosphere is formal, with tuxedo-clad waiters who provide exquisite service, the atmosphere is never stuffy. You'll find the Tack Room near Sabino Canyon, in an elegant, historic hacienda that was built in 1938. Before dinner, or after, you can relax by the fireplace in the restaurant's comfortable lounge.

The fare at this extraordinary restaurant is deserving of its fine reputation. Appetizers may include dried beef tenderloin machaca baked in puffed pastry and served on a bed of jicama, papaya, and black bean relish, or shrimp and crab tamales with roasted garlic and banana sauce. When your appetite has been properly primed, your server will deliver a light and fruity sorbet to help you make a smooth transition to your entree. Main dish menu options comprise such traditional favorites as pork tenderloin marinated in mustard and sour mash bourbon, and Arizona four pepper steak. Desserts are smooth and elegant; the chocolate mousse with pecans in Frangelico cream is irresistible. And, just when you think your meal has drawn to a close, truffles and long-stemmed roses for the ladies are slipped onto your table.

Caruso's

Address: 434 N. 4th Ave.

Phone: 520-624-5765

Hours: Tu-Sat 4:30 p.m. to 10 p.m., Sunday 4 p.m. to 10 p.m.

Remarks: $$, S, NS, CC, CH, RS for large parties, Beer and Wine, P

A popular restaurant that has been in business since the '30s, Caruso's specializes in Southern Italian cooking. Luxurious lasagna, shrimp marinara, and fettuccine al pesto are among the restaurant's exceptional offerings. The spacious patio is a wonderful place to satisfy your hunger after a day of shopping on the nearby historic Fourth Avenue, to sip a glass of wine as you watch passers-by, or to rest your weary feet and enjoy one of the Caruso's signature pizzas after exploring the town.

Bazil's

Address: 4777 E. Sunrise Dr.

Phone: 520-577-3322 or 520-577-1100 (for to-go orders)

Hours: M-Sun 5 p.m. to 10 p.m.

Remarks: $$$, S, NS, CC, RS, FB

Delicious – and large – portions are the signatures of Bazil's. Every meal comes with a salad and soup to start, so you'd better be hungry. Although the focus at Bazil's is largely on Italian fare, the restaurant is widely known to have some of the best steaks in Tucson. New York and Peppercorn steaks are two of the most often-ordered menu items, and chicken Vesuvio, fresh fish, and homemade lasagna are not far behind. The eggplant parmigiana melts in your mouth and pizzas can be ordered to go. Bazil's atmosphere is cozy and softly-lit, with intimate booth seating and excellent service. Just in case you have room for dessert, sweet options include Chocolate Decadence and other fabulous finishes.

Capriccio Ristorante

Address: 4825 N. 1st Ave.

Phone: 520-887-2333

Hours: M-Sat 5:30 p.m. to 9:30 p.m.

Remarks: $$$, S, NS, CC, CH, RS, FB

While the decor at Capriccio Ristorante may be under-stated – with spotless white tablecloths, muted colors on the walls and furnishings, and subtle Mediterranean-style artwork – the delectable fare does anything but blend into the background. The menu is both sophisticated and classic, with specialties that include succulent roast duckling with Grand Marnier and green peppercorn sauce, flavorful and filling pasta creations, veal entrees, and fresh, unusually seasoned seafood dishes.

Daniel's

Address: St. Philip's Plaza, 4340 N. Campbell Ave.

Phone: 520-742-3200

Hours: Lunch 11:30 a.m. to 3 p.m. daily (October-May), Dinner Sun-Th 5 p.m. to 9 p.m., F-Sat 5 p.m. to 11 p.m. year-round

Remarks: $$$$, S, NS, CC, RS, FB, P

When you come to Daniel's, you can expect to enjoy all of the flavors for which Northern Italy is loved, combined with the exceptional service and attention to detail that create a truly elegant dining experience. To begin, you'll be treated with freshly baked bread, such as seasoned foccacia topped with a smooth ricotta cheese spread. The zuppa al frutti di mare – seafood soup in a white wine and leek seafood broth – and Insalata Cesare are two favorite starter dishes. The entrees you'll find here may be some of the best that you will ever taste. We recommend the charbroiled Mahi Mahi garnished with marinated artichoke hearts and the bistecca alla Fiorentina. The pan-seared duck breast is also divine. For dessert, pull out all the stops and order the Torta di Tartufo Liquefatto: individual warm molten chocolate truffle cake with vanilla bean gelato on the side. You'll be glad you did.

Vivace

Address: 4811 E. Grant Rd.
Phone: 520-795-7221
Hours: M-Th 11:30 p.m. to 9 p.m., F-Sat 11:30 a.m. to 10 p.m., Sun 5 p.m. to 9 p.m.
Remarks: $$$, S, NS, CC, CH, RS, FB

The Italian word "vivace" translates into "lively" in English, and when you visit this elegant restaurant by Daniel Scordato, you'll agree that the name was well-chosen. The restaurant has a large open oven that allows you to see Scordato in action as he prepares your meal to order. The menu changes seasonally, and consists of mostly modern Italian cuisine that includes delicious pastas, unusual entrees, and freshly baked foccacia breads. Scordato's pork tenderloin drizzled with a piquant lemon caper sauce and served with vegetable risotto is truly memorable. Grilled eggplant accented with chevre and sundried tomatoes is another outstanding dish. The desserts are exquisite, especially the chocolate polenta cake with a dark chocolate sauce and crème Anglaise.

French, Spanish, and Greek Cuisine

Le Bistro

Address: 2574 N. Campbell Ave.
Phone: 520-327-3086
Hours: M-F 11 a.m. to 2:30 p.m., M-Sun 5 p.m. to closing
Remarks: $$$, S, NS, CC, CH, RS

With a mixture of Art Deco furnishings, lace curtains, and lush green plants, Le Bistro is the picture of a classic French bistro. Both owner and chef, Laurent Reux specializes in French dishes that are innovative and traditional. His ever-changing daily menu includes a number of fresh seafood entrees such as Filet of Salmon in ginger crust, and blackened scallops dressed in a piquant honey jalapeño sauce. Given the true gourmet quality of the cuisine at Le Bistro, you'll find your meal to be well worth the cost.

Encore Med and Café Triana

Address: 2959 N. Swan Rd.
Phone: 520-881-6611
Hours: Encore Med M-Sun 5:30 p.m. to 10:30 p.m.   *Café Triana M-Sun 11:30 a.m. to 11 p.m.*
Remarks: $$$, S, NS, CC, CH, RS, FB, P

The casual, yet elegant Café Triana offers Tucson's only authentic Spanish cuisine. The tapas – both hot and cold – are excellent. Encore Med is more formal and quite lovely, serving up Continental and Spanish cuisine prepared by its internationally trained chef/owner, Pedro Sevilla. Sevilla's entree specialties include such dishes as calamari alla Romana, filet of baby lamb with eucalyptus honey sauce, and duckling Bigarde. The service in both establishments is outstanding.

Olive Tree

Address: 7000 E. Tanque Verde Rd.
Phone: 520-298-1845
Hours: M-Sat 11:30 a.m. to 9 p.m., Sun 5 p.m. to 9 p.m.
Remarks: $$$, S, NS, CC, CH, RS, FB, P

If you have the taste for Greek food in mind, you'll want to head to the Olive Tree. Enhancing the wide variety of palate-pleasing Greek dishes are the restaurant's comfortable environment and pleasant service. With choices such as pan fried calamari, moussaka, dolmades (stuffed grape leaves), and 24 other entrees, you really can't go wrong at the Olive Tree. Whenever possible, we try to secure a spot on the restaurant's tree and flower-lined patio, which is among Tucson's finest outdoor dining atmospheres.

Le Rendez-vous

Address: 3844 E. Ft. Lowell Rd.
Phone: 520-323-7373
Hours: Tu-F 11:30 a.m. to 2 p.m., Tu-Sun 6 p.m. to 10 p.m.
Remarks: $$$$, S, NS, CC, CH, RS, FB

Amid the elegant and intimate setting that characterizes Le Rendez-vous, Chef Jean-Claude Berger creates many classic French favorites. In this carefully remodeled house – complete with two distinctive dining rooms that are furnished with comfortable furnishings and lovely accents – you'll find the service to be professional and warm, the food delightful. Menu items may include such delicacies as canard à l'orange and duck pâté – the daily specials are always enticing – and you'll want to be sure that someone at your table orders the Grand Marnier Soufflé for dessert.

Asian Cuisine

Lotus Garden

Address: 5975 E. Speedway Blvd.

Phone: 520-298-3351

Hours: Sun-Th 11:30 a.m. to 10 p.m., F-Sat 11:30 a.m. to 12 a.m.

Remarks: $$, S, NS, CC, CH, RS, FB, P

Voted Tucson's #1 Chinese restaurant by a local magazine, the Lotus Garden offers some of the city's best Szechwan and Cantonese cuisine. In operation for more than 25 years, the Lotus Garden has cultivated an environment that is at once contemporary and elegant. Specialties include sautéed spicy lobster, lemon chicken, and moo shu vegetables. To add a bit of merriment to your dining experience, enjoy Polynesian drinks or a glass of wine on the patio, and be sure to save room for the interesting desserts that complete the menu.

Sakura Teppan Steak and Sushi

Address: 6534 E. Tanque Verde Rd.

Phone: 520-298-7777

Hours: M-Fri 11 a.m. to 2 p.m., and 5 p.m. to 10 p.m., Sun-Th 5 p.m. to 10 p.m., F-Sat 5 p.m. to 11 p.m.

Remarks: $$$, S, NS, CC, RS, FB

Fresh seafood is flown into Sakura Teppan daily and winds up in some of the best sushi in town. The decor is traditional Japanese and elegant. If you order a Teppan-yaki dish, you'll sit on individual stools around the large iron griddle upon which your meal will be prepared. When you visit Sakura Teppan, prepare to see a show – experienced chefs use razor sharp knives and other utensils in a manner that is breathtakingly bold: searing ingredients, juggling salt and pepper shakers, and executing skillful maneuvers like you've never seen before. This is a great place to celebrate a special occasion, or to turn an ordinary day into extraordinary one.

Vegetarian Fare

Sprouts

Address: 621 N. 4th Ave.

Phone: 520-620-1938

Hours: Sun-Th 11 a.m. to 9 p.m., F-Sat 11 a.m. to 10 p.m.

Remarks: $, NS, CC, CH

Finally... Tucson has a strictly-vegetarian restaurant, and it's a good one. While the menu is not too extensive, every choice is a winner. The greens are all organic, fresh, and bursting with flavor, and the Seitan Fajitas are incredible. Portions are very generous, but if you have a huge appetite, you can also fill up on some delicious fruit smoothies. The atmosphere is casual and charming.

Cafés and Coffee Houses

Bailey and Bailey Café

Address: 330 S. Scott Ave., adjacent to the Temple of Music and Art

Phone: 520-792-2623

Hours: M-Sat 7 a.m. to 3 p.m.

Remarks: $, S, NS, CC, RS, P

B&B uses Illy beans from Italy to create some of the finest espresso drinks in town. Lattes, cappuccinos, and mochas are all delicious. In addition to wonderful coffee, B&B has fresh pastries and authentic baguettes. Later in the day, you can enjoy the delicious roasts, exciting salads, and exotic cheeses that are on display for take-out in the case. As an added treat for theater-goers at the Temple of Music and Art, B&B will also serve dinner on the evening of every performance.

Epic Café

Address: 745 N. 4th Ave.	

Address: 745 N. 4th Ave.

Phone: 520-624-6844

Hours: M-Sun 7 a.m. to 11 p.m., 7 a.m. to 10 p.m. during the summer

Remarks: $, Smoking on Patio Only, CH

Excellent espresso drinks are made using excellent coffee, and Epic Café is another place you'll find those great Illy beans. Combine the coffee with fresh-baked muffins, pastries, and bagels for a perfect snack or breakfast. The Soup of the Day with a fresh baguette makes a perfect light lunch. The decor is modern and creative with large windows and a comfy couch. Even the bathroom is wild and fun. Outside, tables line the sidewalks, so you can choose to sit the shade or the sun.

Café Paraiso

Address: 800 E. University Blvd.

Phone: 520-624-1707

Hours: M-Sun 7 a.m. to 11 p.m., 7 a.m. to 9 p.m. during the summer)

Remarks: $, Smoking on Patio Only, CC, CH, P

This is a cozy little place near the U of A campus, with a warming fireplace that's reminiscent of the coffeehouses of old. Wing-back chairs invite you to sink in with outstanding espresso drinks, and more than a few good stories have been written on the café's numerous tables. The service here is excellent, and the sandwich choices are also very tasty and generous.

Cuppuccino's Coffee House

Address: 3400 E. Speedway Blvd.

Phone: 520-323-7205

Hours: M-Th 7 a.m. to 11 p.m., Fri 7 a.m. to 12 a.m., Sat 8 a.m. to 12 a.m., Sun 8 a.m. to 5:30 p.m.

Remarks: $, Smoking on Patio Only, CC, CH, P

Cuppuccino's coffee is excellent, their service is efficient, and the salads, sandwiches, and tasty baked goods are always fresh. The decor is modern, with stone-topped tables, shining cement floors and high beamed ceilings that give the coffeehouse a distinctly urban twist. The many windows that surround the eating area let you keep an eye on what's going on outside.

Milagro

Address: 3073 N. Campbell Ave.	
Phone: 520-795-1700	
Hours: M-Sat 7 a.m. to 11 p.m.	
Remarks: $, Smoking on Patio Only, CC, CH, RS, P	

Quality espresso drinks are available at Milagro. Menu items include baked goods – scones are especially delicious – or you can feast on sandwiches, salads, and light dishes. The decor is tasteful with lovely wrought iron tables and chairs.

Fast Food

Pronto

Address: 2955 E. Speedway Blvd.	
Phone: 520-326-9707	
Hours: Sun-Th 11 a.m. to 9 p.m., F-Sat 11 a.m. to 10 p.m.	
Remarks: $, Smoking on Patio Only, CC, CH, Beer and Wine, P	

This is Italian fast food, and quite possibly the best fast food in town. The prices are more than reasonable. Great dishes include the homemade lasagna and the grilled vegetable sandwich with caramelized onions on foccacia. Generous espresso drinks and pastries are also available.

Baggin's

Address: Pima/Craycroft	
Phone: 520-795 – 7135	
Address: Church/Pennington	
Phone: 520-792-1344	
Address: Speedway/Treat	
Phone: 520-327-4342	
Address: Campbell/Ft. Lowell	
Phone: 520-327-1611	

Address: Broadway/Rosemont	
Phone: 520-327-8718	
Address: Oracle/Orange Grove	
Phone: 520-575-8878	

Baggin's food is made from scratch daily. Their made-to-order sandwich options include turkey, chicken, beef, ham, cheese, and vegetarian, all dressed to your specifications and served on your choice of freshly baked breads. A variety of delicious salads round out the menu. A nice touch is the chocolate chip cookie that comes with each sandwich.

Sanchez Burrito Company

Address: 2530 N. 1st Ave.
Phone: 520-622-2092
Address: 1350 Wetmore Rd.
Phone: 520-887-0955
Address: 2526 E. Broadway (seating very limited)
Phone: 520-795-3306
Address: 1060 N. Craycroft Rd. (full service restaurant)
Phone: 520-747-0901
Address: 5601 E. 22nd St. "Sanchez Jr."   *(owned by the same family and has a similar menu.)*
Phone: 520-748-8103

"Sanch" is an old favorite of many Tucsonans. Each location offers large burritos over the counter, all-you-can-eat freshly made tortilla chips, and take-out or eat in service that's friendly and quick. All burritos can be ordered "Sanchez style," complete with sour cream and guacamole, and a great vegetarian burrito is available – just ask for number 11. Tucson locals say the best way to approach your burrito is from the top; cut it open, stir up the ingredients, and enjoy. Be sure to grab lots of napkins!

Accommodations in Tucson vary from world-class, full-service hotels and resorts to unique B&Bs in historic neighborhoods to guest ranches located just minutes from downtown. Budget travelers will also find plenty of lodging options to suit their needs. Your decision on where to stay will depend on how much you want to spend and what area of Tucson will serve you best.

The time of year you visit may also affect your choice of accommodations. If you visit Tucson during the summer months, you'll be pleasantly surprised by the low rates, which can be 40% off winter rates, or more. Each establishment has its own set of seasonal rate periods, so you'll be wise to inquire at each place you call about the particular dates you plan to visit. Please note that taxes are not included in the room rates.

The Westin La Paloma

Address: 3800 E. Sunrise Dr., Tucson, AZ 85718

Phone: 520-742-6000, 1-800-876-3683

Rates: From $190 to $1,500 in the winter, and $80 to $800 in the summer for accommodations that range from single rooms to deluxe suites.

Facilities: 27-hole golf course, 12 lighted tennis courts, pool, 3 spas, health club, aerobics room, indoor racquetball, croquet and volleyball courts, jogging trails, children's lounge and daycare center.

Services: 5 restaurants, 2 bars, 24-hour room service, shopping shuttle, bike rental.

Located in Tucson's Catalina foothills, La Paloma offers a panoramic view of the high Sonoran Desert and the nearby Santa Catalina Mountains. The resort is surrounded by the extraordinary beauty of the desert's native vegetation, and the grounds bloom with carefully attended gardens that complement the hotel's Mission-style setting. Rooms and suites have comfortable furnishings and Southwestern decor, and include sitting areas, fully stocked refrigerators, and private patios or balconies.

La Paloma's 27-hole golf course offers abundant challenge for golf enthusiasts of all levels, and the resort's many lighted tennis courts allow you to play well into the evening. Racquetball, aerobics, and croquet are among the other recreational options available at La Paloma, and the professionals at the child care center can see to it that you have some worry-free time away from the kids.

The five restaurants at La Paloma offer a variety of cuisines, and have been designed to create a relaxing, contemporary atmosphere. The Desert Garden is the hotel's main dining room, which features Mediterranean fare and scenic views of the Santa Catalina Mountains. La Villa's Southwestern-style ha-

The Westin La Paloma with the Santa Catalina Mountains in the background.

Courtesy The Westin La Paloma

cienda specializes in fresh seafood dishes. If you just want a snack, try the Courtside Deli, or Sabinos, the pool-side bar, for a tasty hamburger or hot dog. For more formal dining, put on your jacket and head to the La Paloma Dining Room at the La Paloma Country Club to enjoy some of Tucson's finest gourmet American cuisine. If you happen to be in town on New Year's Eve, you can waltz the night away with the Tucson Symphony in the resort's grand ballroom.

Canyon Ranch Resort

Address: 8600 E. Rockcliff Rd., Tucson, AZ 85715

Phone: 520-749-9000, 1-800-726-9900

Rates: Call for details.

Facilities: 62,000 sq. ft. spa complex with 7 gymnasiums, squash and racquetball courts, yoga/meditation dome, locker rooms with sauna, steam, and inhalation rooms, Jacuzzis, private sun-bathing areas, 8 lighted tennis courts, 1 indoor pool, 3 outdoor pools, Health & Healing Center staffed with medical and related health professionals.

Services: More than 40 fitness classes, massage, hydro massage, sports and fitness instruction, and special programs that address a variety of issues.

One of the country's premier health spas, Canyon Ranch Resort is one of two year-round resorts that Mel and Enid Zuckerman have founded to promote healthy living. The second resort is located in Massachusetts' Berkshire mountains, and both of these internationally-acclaimed resorts have been named "Best Spa" by readers of *Condé Nast Traveler* magazine.

Since Canyon Ranch opened its doors in 1979, it has helped thousands of guests – including many well-known celebrities – fulfill their desires to create healthier and more rewarding lifestyles. Located in the foothills of the Santa Catalina Mountains, this extraordinary vacation resort offers guests more than 40 fitness classes, personalized hiking and biking regimens, plus individual consultation and workshops designed to aid in stress management and the promotion of guests' overall well-being. Professional assistance with disease prevention, smoking cessation, nutrition improvement, and weight loss is also available.

The remarkably high 3:1 staff to guest ratio ensures that you'll have the support you need to meet any goals you may have for your visit. The resort's top-quality cadre of medical doctors, nurses, psychologists and counselors, exercise physiologists, fitness instructors, registered dietitians, movement therapists, tennis and racquetball pros, aestheticians, massage therapists, and support staff will attend to your every need. Healthy cooking classes, yoga, tai chi, and meditation classes, and periodic programs that focus on such issues as health, aging and recovery from life's myriad traumas are also available.

The accommodations at Canyon Ranch include single-story adobe-style cottages that can house up to 200 guests. A newly-renovated Spanish Colonial-style clubhouse is where you'll find the front desk, guest services office, meeting rooms, boutique, and common dining room. Nearby are the Demonstration Kitchen and Creative Arts Center. These carefully constructed and well-maintained buildings are surrounded by acres of cactus gardens, exotic flowers, and tropical trees. Running streams, quiet pools, and fountains add to the richness of the landscaping, and the trail-strewn desert lies beyond.

Westward Look Resort

Address: 245 East Ina Rd., Tucson, AZ 85704
Phone: 520-297-1151, 1-800-722-2500
Rates: From $169 to $269 in the winter, and $109 to $179 in the summer for accommodations that range from single rooms to deluxe suites.
Facilities: 8 tennis courts ($8/hr fee), 3 pools, 3 whirlpool spas, fitness center, jogging trail, volleyball, basketball, softball, horseshoes, aerobics room, pro shop.
Services: 2 restaurants, cocktail lounge, room service, tennis lessons.

This beautifully landscaped, 80-acre resort originally opened in 1929 as a dude ranch. Overlooking the Tucson valley and the Santa Catalina Mountains, the 244-room hotel enhances its Southwestern feel with exposed-beam ceilings, expansive windows, and softly colorful furnishings. While rooms vary in decor and layout, they all come extra-large, and have private patios or balconies. Other amenities include complimentary coffee service, a mini-refrigerator and stocked service bar, an iron and ironing board.

There's plenty of fun to be had at Westward Look, whether you're traveling alone or with your family. You can swim in the pool or traverse the resort's jogging trails, take an aerobics class or engage in a pick-up game of basketball or volleyball. Improve your tennis game with lessons given by the resort's tennis pros, or simply relax with a round of horseshoes or a good book.

The resort's Gold Room restaurant gives you a sweeping, panoramic view of Tucson to enjoy while you partake of the chef's exceptional traditional Continental cuisine and seafood specialties. In the Lookout Bar & Grille, you'll find a more casual atmosphere and delicious light Southwestern fare. The bar also has recorded and live entertainment in the evenings.

Sheraton El Conquistador Resort and Country Club

Address: 10000 N. Oracle Rd., Tucson, AZ 85737

Phone: 520-544-5000, 1-800-325-7832

Rates: From $174 to $330 for accommodations that range from single rooms to deluxe suites.

Facilities: 2 18-hole golf courses, 1 9-hole golf course, 31 lighted tennis courts, 4 swimming pools, 7 indoor racquetball courts, spas, volleyball, basketball, 2 health clubs.

Services: 5 restaurants, 24-hour room service, shopping shuttle, airport shuttle ($21/person one way), car rental, tour desk, stables, bike rentals.

Everything at this Sheraton resort has been done on a grand scale, with an exceptional attention to detail that leaves nothing to be desired. Whether you're after idyllic scenery, a good game of golf or tennis, a visit to the Santa Catalina Mountains on horseback, or just relaxing, El Conquistador can – and will – provide it. Set at the end of the Catalina Mountain range, this 434-room oasis combines the influences of Native American, Spanish, and Mexican architecture. The sunsets here are spectacular. Each rooms has a balcony or patio with a view of the desert, the mountains, or the pool and courtyard.

The five restaurants at El Conquistador allow you to experience a

The Courtyard pool at Sheraton El Conquistador.

Courtesy of Sheraton El Conquistador Resort

variety of culinary experiences during your stay. The Sundance has been recognized as having "Tucson's Best Sunday Brunch" by locals. The White Dove is an informal, contemporary cafe that offers healthy and delicious Southwestern fare, while highlights at La Vista include flavorful Continental cuisine and memorable mountain views. For fine Mexican dining, and live mariachi music, visit Dos Locos Cantina. The Last Territory Steakhouse and Dance Hall is a good place to take the whole family. The restaurant serves open-flame mesquite steaks, seafood, chicken, and ribs, complemented by live country and western music on most evenings.

Waterfalls in front of the main entrance of Loews Ventana Canyon Resort.

Courtesy of Loews Ventana Canyon Resort

Loews Ventana Canyon Resort

Address: 7000 N. Resort Dr., Tucson, AZ 85715

Phone: 520-299-2020, 1-800-223-0888

Rates: From $295 to $950 in the winter, and $89 to $195 in the summer for accommodations that range from single rooms to deluxe suites.

Facilities: 18-hole golf course, 10 lighted tennis courts, 2 swimming pools, health club, spa, croquet green, fitness trails, aerobics room, steam room.

Services: 5 restaurants, lakeside nightclub, 24-hour room service, shopping shuttle, car rental, mountain bike rental.

With 93 acres of arid desert land situated atop a plateau in Ventana Canyon, this luxury resort is accented by the beauty of saguaro cactus and mesquite trees of the surrounding Sonoran Desert. The decor in Ventana's 400 rooms accentuates the desert atmosphere by incorporating pastels and sunset tones into wall and window coverings and furnishings. Room amenities include a fully stocked refrigerator, mini-bar, and three conveniently located telephones.

In addition to the many recreational opportunities available at Ventana – including championship golf, swimming, and tennis – there is also good hiking on, and just adjacent to, the resort's property. This is one of the few places you'll see a rare specimen of saguaro cactus known as a "crown saguaro." You can identify this unique saguaro by its crown-shaped top. Ask the concierge for more details on where to hike, and remember: wear sunscreen and take water, even on a short trip.

A favorite of Tucsonans and visitors alike, Loews Ventana restaurant serves a large selection of nouvelle American cuisine, and most tables have a good view of Tucson. The Canyon Cafe is their more informal dining area, and serves breakfast, lunch, and dinner. If dining by a small lake is appealing to you, check out The Flying V Bar and Grill, which offers Southwestern fare, steaks, and seafood. Later in the evening, the Grill is transformed into a disco that's a favorite of locals, too. For grilled hamburgers and chicken, and fresh salads, snacks, and sandwiches, try Bill's Grill, located by the pool.

Tucson National Golf & Conference Resort

Address: 2727 W. Club Dr., Tucson, AZ 85741
Phone: 520-297-2271, 1-800-528-4856
Rates: From $265 to $350 in the winter, and $85 to $120 in the summer for accommodations that range from single rooms to deluxe suites.
Facilities: USGA 27-hole golf course, swimming pool, 2 tennis courts, complete health spa, pro shop, volleyball court, basketball court, aerobics room, steam room, whirlpool spa, sauna.
Services: 3 restaurants and 1 bar, 24-hour room service, exercise classes.

True to its name, Tucson National Golf and Conference Resort specializes in providing championship-quality golf and top-notch conference facilities to business and leisure travelers from around the world. In fact, the resort has hosted the Northern Telecom Open in 17 of the last 29 years.

The 167-room, Mission-style hotel offers spacious accommodations that draw upon the muted colors of the

Southwest to create a relaxing and contemporary decor. Private patios overlook the resort's carefully groomed fairways and sparkling lakes. If you need some restorative care, take advantage of Tucson National's full-service health spa that offers everything from manicures and pedicures to Swedish massages, herbal wraps, loofah scrubs, and thoroughly decadent Salt Glows.

Enjoy fine dining at the Catalina Grille, where the emphasis of the main menu – featuring Sonoran, Italian, and other regional cuisines – changes weekly. The restaurant is open for dinner every day except Sunday, and reservations and jackets are required. In Fiesta Room and Bar, stylized copper tables and chandeliers reminiscent of Arizona's copper mining history contribute to the restaurant's Southwestern ambience. The Fiesta Room is open for three meals and into the evening, and the more casual Legends is a popular sports bar and grill that offers lunch and dinner as well.

Hotels

Arizona Inn

Address: 2200 E. Elm St., Tucson, AZ 85719

Phone: 520-325-1541, 1-800-933-1093

Rates: From $122 to $195 and up in the fall, and $104 to $184 and up in the summer for accommodations that range from single rooms to deluxe suites. Rates are slightly higher during the winter months.

Facilities: 2 Har-Tru tennis courts, swimming pool, croquet, table tennis, library.

Services: Restaurant, room service.

Occupying 14 acres in the heart of Tucson, this 80-room historical hotel is an elegant and peaceful family retreat. Built in 1930, the pink stucco buildings in the enclosed courtyard are connected by walkways that meander through the inn's flowering gardens. The rooms are individually decorated with careful attention to detail, some have fireplaces and most have private patios.

The hotel's concierge can help you with reservations or transportation to many of the area's restaurants, shops, and attractions. Back at the hotel, you can sun yourself by the pool, or engage in a civilized round of croquet or table tennis. The well-stocked library is a great place to relax with a book by the fire, or converse with other guests.

The historic Arizona Inn.

The restaurant is open to the public, and serves three delicious and well-presented meals daily. Cuisine is traditional or Continental with a Southwestern touch. The dinner menu changes monthly, and includes such favorites as filet mignon, succulent lamb, and fresh salmon. There's also a monthly "Celebration Menu," with a special regional theme. In the evenings, you can enjoy refreshments and live music in the Audubon Lounge.

Embassy Suites-Tucson/Broadway

Address: 5335 E. Broadway Blvd., Tucson, AZ 85711

Phone: 520-745-2700, 1-800-362-2779

Rates: From $139 in the winter to $95 in the summer.

Facilities: Swimming pool, whirlpool spa, sauna, gas grills.

Services: Room service, complimentary evening cocktails, complimentary health club passes.

This Mission-style hotel is an all-suite inn located in the eastern part of downtown. Arranged around the hotel's garden atrium and pool, the spacious suites are furnished with sofa beds and can accommodate up to six people. The suites also have fully-equipped kitchenettes so you can do some cooking for yourself, if you like.

With the exception of the made-to-order breakfast your hosts will prepare for you – or your own home-cooking – most of your dining will be done off the premises, as there is no restaurant at the Embassy Suites. As a special treat, the lounge offers a complimentary extended happy hour to hotel guests every evening.

Windmill Inn at St. Philip's Plaza

Address: 4250 N. Campbell, Tucson, AZ 85718

Phone: 520-577-0007, 1-800-547-4747

Rates: From $123 in the winter to $79 in the summer.

Facilities: Swimming pool, whirlpool spa, laundry.

Services: Continental breakfast, morning paper, lending library, dry cleaning service, bicycle use.

Overlooking the Rillito River Wash a few miles north of downtown, the Windmill Inn is a nice, moderately priced hotel that offers spacious suites with many amenities for the business or vacationing traveler. All rooms come with desks, couches, three phones, two TVs, a small refrigerator, and microwave.

A lending library has all the latest bestsellers for you to enjoy during your stay, and bicycles are available for both adults and children. Just across the street is the Rillito River bike path, where you can ride, take a morning run, or a leisurely walk in the evening.

You needn't go far to find fine dining or shopping, as St. Philip's Plaza has three top-notch restaurants and many interesting shops that warrant exploration. See the *Shopping* and *Restaurant* sections for more information on the offerings in St. Philip's Plaza.

The Hotel Congress located in downtown Tucson.

Courtesy of Hotel Congress

Hotel Congress

Address: 311 E. Congress St., Tucson, AZ 85701

Phone: 520-622-8848, 1-800-722-8848

Rates: From $43 in the winter to $40 in the summer. Call for details on hostel rooms.

Built in the days when the railroad was king of the transportational realm, this 40-room historic hotel is centrally located near the city's art district and downtown. Adjacent to the Amtrak, Greyhound, and the downtown Sun Tran bus terminals, the hotel is run as a budget hotel and youth hostel. This charismatic establishment earned its place in the history of the West in 1934, when police officials apprehended John Dillinger's gang in Tucson while registered in one of Hotel Congress' rooms upstairs.

Both the lobby and guest rooms reflect a unique Southwestern flair, and all accommodations have private bathrooms with either bathtubs or showers. Special rates are given to students, and it's less expensive still to rent a hostel room (read: shared). The hotel has a cafe and Western bar, and is also home to Club Congress, a popular dance club and live music venue. (See the listing in the *Arts & Entertainment* section for details.)

Bed and Breakfast Inns

The SunCatcher

Address: 105 N. Avenida Javalina, Tucson, AZ 85748
Phone: 1-800-835-8012, in Arizona call 520-885-0883
Innkeeper: David Williams
Rates: $140 to $165 double, $25 extra person.
Comments: Two-night minimum stay.

Set on four lovely acres just outside of Tucson, this four-room bed and breakfast offers many of the luxuries and amenities that one would expect only in the finest hotels. The traditional decor is professionally designed, and creates a warm and welcoming atmosphere for the visiting guest. If you want some exercise, the inn has a heated pool, spa, and tennis courts, and the adjacent Saguaro National Park has hiking trails that wind through miles of the desert's most striking scenery.

Each room at the inn is named after one of the worlds four "great" hotels – The Connaught in London, The Regent in Hong Kong, The Four Seasons in Chicago, and The Oriental in Bangkok – and each is decorated in a style representative of its namesake.

Breakfast options include fresh fruit and cereal, an innovative entree that's made-to-order, or both. Plenty of fruit juice and fresh coffee help you feel prepared for your day of exploration or relaxation.

Catalina Park Inn

Address: 309 E. 1st St., Tucson, AZ 85705	
Phone: 520-792-4541, 1-800-792-4885	
Innkeepers: Mark Hall and Paul Richard	
Rates: $90 to $130, double, $15 extra person.	
Comments: Complimentary breakfast and morning newspaper.	

Constructed in 1927, the Catalina Park Inn is well-known for its atmosphere of comfort, elegance, and style. Located just a few blocks north of downtown, this spacious estate has four guest rooms, with a traditional decor and relaxed environment that will ensure that you feel right at home.

Each of the rooms – The Cottage, The Oak Room and The East Room and West Room – has a private bath, television, telephone, and other convenient amenities. While The Cottage has a private garden and covered terrace, The Oak Room is more spacious and gives you a great view of the mountains and Tucson's incomparable sunrise. Both the East and West Rooms have a bedroom and a sitting room, and a furnished balcony from which you can survey Catalina Park.

A fresh Continental breakfast and a newspaper are the first order of every day. You may enjoy your meal in the breakfast room that overlooks the garden, or have it delivered to your door to be enjoyed in the privacy of your room.

Catalina Park Inn.

Courtesy of Catalina Park Inn

Casa Tierra

Address: 11155 W. Calle Pima, Tucson, AZ 85743
Phone: 520-578-3058
Innkeepers: Lyle and Karen Hymer-Thompson
Rates: $65 to $75, double.
Comments: Two-night minimum stay on weekends.

Located just west of Tucson, Casa Tierra exemplifies the haciendas of old central Mexico. Built on five acres in the Sonoran desert, the all-adobe house was designed and constructed by the innkeepers themselves, and features latilla and viga ceilings, brick floors, patterned Talavera tile, and Mexican furnishings.

The three guest rooms all have private baths, separate entrances, and patios. Rooms open into a common court-yard where you can relax with a glass of iced tea, catch up on your correspondence, or discuss your expeditions to the nearby Arizona-Sonora Desert Museum and the Saguaro National Park West with other guests. At the end of the day, you may want to melt into the outdoor Jacuzzi and enjoy the sunset before heading out to dinner.

Casa Tierra serves a full breakfast that begins with fresh coffee or tea, and includes fruit juices and home-baked goods. You may enjoy your meal in the dining area or in your room.

La Posada Del Valle

Address: 1640 N. Campbell Ave., Tucson, AZ 85719
Phone: 520-795-3840
Innkeepers: Debbi and Charles Bryant
Rates: $90 to $125, double.
Comments: Complimentary breakfast and afternoon tea.

Built in 1929 from designs created by renowned Tucson architect, Josias T. Joesler, La Posada del Valle's architecture is reminiscent of the early Sante Fe style. The inn is com-prised of two spacious suites and three large guest rooms, and is conveniently located across the street from the University of Arizona Hospital and just a few blocks from the U of A campus. True to the style of the era in which it was built, the inn is furnished with antiques and Art Deco pieces from the 1920s and '30s.

Each of the rooms is named after a well-known American woman, including such figures as Isadora Duncan and Sophie Tucker, and is furnished with stately antiques from the early 1900s. King, queen, and twin beds are available – offering flexibility for families, or singles traveling together – and all have private baths and entrances. The breakfasts here are gourmet, and include homebaked breads, flavorful quiches, and plenty of fresh fruit.

Peppertrees Bed and Breakfast Inn

Address: 742 E. University Ave., Tucson, AZ 85719

Phone: 520-622-7167, 1-800-348-5763

Innkeeper: Marjorie Martin

Rates: $88, double, guesthouse $150.

Comments: Complimentary breakfast and afternoon tea.

Fully restored and furnished with antique pieces from England, this 1905 Victorian-style house is named for the two large California pepper trees that once grew in front of the inn. Located within a stone's throw of the University of Arizona, the inn is also an easy walk from the Arizona Historical Society Museum, the Flandrau Science Center, the Old Pueblo Trolley Line, and many other downtown attractions.

Peppertrees has three rooms, each with a private bath, and two two-bedroom guest houses. The guest houses are equiped with full kitchens, laundry facilities, private patios, phones, and televisions.

The inn provides a full gourmet breakfast, and Marjorie has published two popular cookbooks, including *Recipes from Peppertrees* and *Breakfast at Peppertrees*.

Casa Alegre

Address: 316 E. Speedway Blvd., Tucson, AZ 85705
Phone: 520-628-1800, 1-800-628-5654
Innkeeper: Phyllis Florek
Rates: $80 to $95, double.
Comments: Weekly, corporate, and senior citizen rates available.

A relaxed and comfortable atmosphere, this 1915 Craftsman bungalow is an architectural celebration of Tucson's historical past. Located within minutes of downtown, and in walking distance to the University of Arizona, Casa Alegre's decor and furnishings reflect the history of Old Tucson.

Each of the inn's four rooms reflect a particular historical theme that gives them an individual charm. All rooms have private baths, and a television and telephone are available for your use in the common Arizona Room. When you return from your adventures, you can stave off the heat with a swim in the pool, or just relax on the patio by the mesquite and flower-fringed fountain. A full breakfast centered around a fresh, signature entree is served each morning, with seasonal fruit, juices and home-baked breads on the side.

The Adobe Rose Inn

Address: 940 N. Olsen Ave., Tucson, AZ 85719
Phone: 520-318-4644
Innkeeper: Diana Graham
Rates: $95 to $115, double
Comments: Senior citizen rates available, not suitable for children.

Originally built in 1933, The Adobe Rose Inn incorporates all of the architectural features that characterize Southwestern design. Burnished oak floors, adobe walls that are one foot thick, and furnishings hewn from native lodgepole pine will give you the feeling of being transported back to Tucson's early years. Within blocks of the university, and minutes of downtown, the inn is a great place to stay, whether you're in town for business or for pleasure.

The Adobe Rose has three rooms in the main house, and two spacious rooms in cottages that are separate from the inn. All rooms have private baths and televisions. The "Sun Flare" cottage has a well-equipped kitchen galley, making it the ideal accommodation for extended stays during which you may want to cook for yourself. A full breakfast is included in your room rate, and consists of a variety of entrees. The inn will accommodate any special dietary requirements with some advance notice.

Rimrock West Hacienda

Address: 3450 N. Drake Place, Tucson, AZ 85749	
Phone: 520-749-8774	
Innkeepers: Val and Mae Robbins	
Rates: $95 to $140, double.	
Comments: Complimentary breakfast.	

Rimrock West's 20-acre Southwestern-style hacienda is located northeast of Tucson, and was created with the intent to provide "scenery and solitude" to visiting guests. Near Sabino Canyon, Mt. Lemmon, and Saguaro National Park East, this comfortable bed and breakfast inn is a great jumping-off place for outstanding area hiking, skiing, and urban exploration.

The three rooms in the Main Hacienda have private baths and televisions, and open onto a hacienda-style courtyard, complete with a fountain. If you're interested in having a little more privacy, there is a separate adobe guest house available that has a full kitchen, fireplace, and private patio. A refreshing swimming pool takes the edge off the heat.

Breakfast is an informal affair at the inn. With your choice of cereals, eggs, pancakes, toast, and muffins to enjoy with a mug of hot coffee or tea, you'll find all the fuel you need for adventures large and small.

Elysian Grove Market

Address: 400 W. Simpson, Tucson, AZ 85701	
Phone: 520-628-1522	
Innkeeper: Deborah Lachapelle	
Rates: $65 to $75, double.	
Comments: Complimentary breakfast, no smoking.	

You'll find this bed and breakfast in a charming old adobe in the Historic Barrio District. Originally built in the 1920s as a corner market – an origin reflected today by the inn's evocative name – the Elysian Grove Market has been care-

Suzanne Myal

The Elysian Grove Market Bed and Breakfast in the Barrio Historico District.

fully renovated into a Southwestern-style inn. The yard and garden are lush and well-maintained, and offer a peaceful place for you to visit with friends or become reacquainted with your loved one or yourself. Furnished with a large selection of Mexican folk art and antiques pieces – many of which are for sale – the inn is a quick drive (or longish walk) from the Tucson Art Museum and many interesting shops, cafés, and galleries.

Guest rooms occupy two separate buildings. The smaller accommodation has two bedrooms that share a bath and a lovely common area. In the larger unit, you'll find two comfortable bedrooms, a large kitchen equipped with full cooking facilities, and a shared bath and common area. Both common areas have telephones and fireplaces. Breakfast includes Latin American coffee, freshly made *empanadas* from the local market, and a variety of fresh fruits.

Dude Ranches

If you're hankering to experience a bit of the cowboy life, a stay at one of Tucson's dude ranches is a great way to fulfill your desires. While most dude ranches don't provoke the high drama of the movie, *City Slickers*, they all offer a unique slice of the Western lifestyle, with daily horseback rides, hikes, cookouts, and scenic views of the desert. These modern dude ranches are designed much like deluxe hotels, with swimming pools, spas, and various other amenities to help you relax and enjoy your surroundings. Most serve three meals a day, and in some cases, meals are included in your room rate.

Some ranches have a minimum stay requirement of one week, and others will take in overnight or weekend guests. The high season is generally from mid-December until early summer, with the more affordable low season continuing through the summer until early winter. We have included four of the best ranches in the area, but if you would like further information on dude ranches, you can contact the Dude Ranchers Association by mail at P.O. Box 471, LaPorte, CO 80535, or call 303-493-7623.

Circle Z Ranch

Address: P.O. Box 194L, Patagonia, AZ 85624

Phone: 520-287-2091

Rates: $159 per person, per night during high season; $131 per person, per night during low season.

Located in the foothills of the Santa Rita Mountains, Circle Z Ranch claims to be the oldest continuously operated dude ranch in Arizona. In keeping with its authentic Western atmosphere, the 5,000-acre ranch also earns a portion of its income by maintaining cattle.

Open to visitors from October through May, the Circle Z Ranch offers horseback riding along a wide variety of trails that suit both the novice and the more advanced rider. Seven Spanish adobe cottages contain individual rooms and spacious suites for guest accommodation. You may also reserve an entire cottage for larger parties or greater privacy. All units have a porch or patio. Guest rooms are not equipped with televisions or phones.

Lazy K Bar Ranch

Address: 8401 N. Scenic Dr., Tucson, AZ 85743

Phone: 520-744-3050

Rates: $145 per person, per night during high season; $115 per person, per night during low season.

This small ranch is suitable for everyone, from singles to families, and prides itself on providing a friendly and informal atmosphere. The ranch is located in the Tucson Mountains, and offers horseback riding every day except Sunday.

Twenty-three comfortable guest rooms are housed in eight cottages and, like the Circle Z, the Lazy K Bar Ranch does not have televisions or phones in guest rooms. Lazy K Bar Ranch is open year-round.

Horseback riders following a desert trail at the Lazy K Bar Ranch.

Tanque Verde Guest Ranch

Address: 14301 E. Speedway Blvd., Tucson, AZ 85748

Phone: 520-296-6275

Rates: $235 per person, per night during high season; $190 per person, per night during low season.

Set in the midst of three ranges – the Rincon, the Catalina, and the Tanque Verde Mountains – Tanque Verde Guest Ranch touts itself as "the last luxurious outpost," and has been featured in *Country Inns and Backroads, Travel and Leisure,* and *Harper's Bazaar* magazines to name a few. Sixty-five guest rooms and suites featuring authentic Southwestern decor are available in the main ranch house or in private *casitas*, and most accommodations have private patios and fireplaces. In addition to horseback riding, Tanque Verde offers a number of activities geared towards environmental awareness, such as its bird banding program, and provides nature hikes guided by a full-time naturalist. Tanque Verde Guest Ranch is open year-round.

Lounging in the lobby of the Tanque Verde Guest Ranch.

White Stallion Ranch

Address: 9251 W. Twin Peaks Rd., Tucson, AZ 85743

Phone: 520-297-0252, 1-800-782-5546

Rates: $134 per person, per night during high season; $125 per person, per night during low season.

Covering 3,000 acres in the Tucson Mountains, White Stallion Ranch is located in an area that epitomizes the beauty of the Southwest. In fact, much of the movie *High Chaparral* was filmed here. The ranch offers both slow and rigorous horseback rides for the equine enthusiast, and puts on a rodeo once a week for ranch guests. The White Stallion Ranch has 29 guest rooms; deluxe suites have fireplaces, whirlpool tubs, and king-sized beds. White Stallion Ranch is open from October through April. Make your reservations early, as many guests make it a point to return every year.

Shopping

To help you make the most of your Tucson shopping experience, we've included only stores that are unique to this area in the following listings. If you want a taste of the Tucson mall scene, check out the ever-burgeoning Tucson Mall at 4500 N. Oracle Road, El Con Mall at 3601 E. Broadway Boulevard, and Park Mall at 5870 E. Broadway Boulevard. Each of these shopping centers has countless department stores, food courts, and other specialty mall shops.

Tucson is a wonderful place to pick up Mexican or Native American goods at prices far lower than those in the Eastern U.S. The selection is better here, too. Tucson's wide variety of ethnic stores also imports art, jewelry, and other goods from all over the world.

The first four shops listed below are located in the warehouse district on Park Avenue, one block east of Euclid Avenue, and one block south of Broadway.

Rustica

Address: 200 S. Park Ave.

Phone: 520-623-4435

Located in an old warehouse near downtown, this family-run business has an ever-changing inventory of products that ranges from fine country-style furniture, including *equipales* (pig-skin items), to knick-knacks of all kinds from Mexico. While you're in the neighborhood, stop at Tooley's Taco Stand just across the street at 299 S. Park Avenue.

Aquí Está

Address: 204 S. Park Ave.

Phone: 520-624-3354

Also located in an old warehouse, Aquí Está specializes in hand-made rustic designs: hand-painted sinks, tile, and furniture. Owner Martha Mendivil and her daughter are ready to assist you with any project – from custom building to tile. If you can't make it down to Nogales, Sonora, this is a great store to wander through to soak up the atmosphere of old Mexico. The store also carries lots of fun accessories that make wonderful gifts.

Madera Designs

Address: 212 S. Park Ave.

Phone: 520-884-9575

Offering authentic antiques and specially manufactured furniture from Mexico, this warehouse shop also has reproductions of *retablos*, *santos*, and furniture from Brazil and Guatemala. Much of the furniture is hand-decorated by local artists.

Magellan Trading

Address: 228 S. Park Ave.

Phone: 520-622-4968

Fourth in the line of warehouse shops, Magellan brings in items from all over the world, including reasonably priced Mexican glassware, Indonesian furniture, African folk art, and wood carvings and weavings from Bali. This store is like a museum; an amazing inventory features items that appeal to both traditional and offbeat sensibilities. And, much like a museum curator, Magellan's knowledgeable manager can fill you in on the history behind your selections.

Berta Wright

Address: 260 E. Congress St., and in the Foothills Mall at 7401 N. La Cholla Blvd.

Phone: Congress – 520-882-7043, Foothills Mall – 520-742-4134

This elegant store showcases works of Southwestern artists as well as international designers and craftsmen. There is a large collection of exotic boxes, Soleri wind bells, sculptures, ceramics, African and Peruvian art, masks, exquisite kimonos, Balinesian and Australian carvings, tapestries... the inventory is too diverse to fully record here. Berta Wright is a wonderful place to purchase a gift for anyone with an interest in art.

Picante Designs

Address: 306 E. Congress St.

Phone: 520-622-8807

Specializing in folk art from Mexico, Picante is a wonderful source of inexpensive and funky treasures, including unusual masks and votive candles. Right next door, and part of the same business, is the nutty Yikes toy store, which carries a conglomeration of kids' toys, books, t-shirts, and silly novelty items.

Old Town Artisans

Address: 186 N. Meyer Ave.

Phone: 520-623-6024

If you're looking for a place to purchase Southwestern art, or would simply like to visit a charming assortment of restored historic adobe buildings, you must visit Old Town Artisans marketplace. Especially worth mentioning is Beth Friedman's Fine Jewelry and Apparel shop, in which you will find a host of outstanding original jewelry created by Beth Friedman and other well-known jewelers. The Old Town Pot Shop carries pottery by Arizona's premier clay artists, and prints and lithographs by R.C. Gorman and other notable artists of the region. Arnold Begay crafts fine silver Navajo jewelry, and specializes in creating custom pieces. The Courthouse Grill can serve you lunch on its Spanish-style patio or indoor restaurant. The grill features mesquite grilled meats as well as standard luncheon fare.

While in the Old Town Artisans area, you may also want to visit the Tucson Museum of Art and Casa Cordova, across the street on N. Meyer Avenue. Casa Cordova is noted for being the oldest free-standing building in Tucson.

The Tucson Museum of Art Gift Shop

Address: 140 N. Main Ave.

Phone: 520-624-2333

This shop is a showcase for local artists and craftspeople. The gifts at the Museum Gift Shop have remained affordable over the years, and there is always a varied selection. Mugs, picture frames, posters, jewelry, woven clothing, and note cards abound here, and a quick stop while downtown is a must.

Morning Star Traders

Address: 2020 E. Speedway Blvd.

Phone: 520-881-2112 or 520-881-6151

The watchword at Morning Star is "authenticity." The owner stocks the store with only the finest Native American treasures, and is quite knowledgeable about both their history and legends.

Kaibab Shops

Address: 2841 N. Campbell Ave.

Phone: 520-795-6905

Specializing in Native American arts and crafts for over forty years, as well as Southwestern furniture and apparel, The Kaibab Shop offers everything from Zuni fetishes and Hopi Kachina dolls to Native American rugs and baskets, as well as the famous Kaibab moccasins.

Turquoise Door

Address: St. Philip's Plaza, 4330 N. Campbell Ave., and at 5675 N. Swan Rd.

Phone: St. Philip's Plaza – 520-299-7787; Swan – 520-299-7551

Established in Tucson more than 16 years ago, this Native American jewelry store carries only top-quality work from superior artists such as Benny and Valerie Aldrige and Arlan Ben. The pieces in their discerning collection of Southwestern jewelry and artwork strike an inspiring balance between the traditional Native American spirit and fresh, contemporary design.

Indian Territory

Address: 5639 N. Swan Rd.

Phone: 520-577-7961

Much like a museum in that it carries both old and new Native American ceremonial regalia, Indian Territory is one of the most interesting shops in Tucson. The shop has a fine collection of authentic Kachinas, fetishes, pottery, dolls, and sculptures. They also carry jewelry, including some old pawn that is especially valued by collectors.

Desert Son

Address: 4759 E. Sunrise Dr.

Phone: 520-299-0818

Desert Son offers an extensive selection of Hopi Kachina dolls, Native American silver and gold jewelry, artwork, hand-made rugs, fetishes, and fine pottery. In this contemporary trading post atmosphere, they also carry custom belts and exceptionally crafted traditional moccasins.

Bahti Indian Arts

Address: St. Philip's Plaza, 4300 N. Campbell Ave.

Phone: 520-577-0290

Bahti is a well-established store with an expansive inventory of authentic Native American weavings, kachinas, jewelry, sand paintings, books, and music. The staff here is both knowledgeable and helpful.

Tierra Madre

Phone: 520-577-1645

Hours: By appointment only; leave a message if no one is home.

One of the many Kachina dolls at Bahti Indian Arts.

For a truly unique shopping experience, schedule a visit to Heidi Baldwin, who sells Mexican antiques and primitive pieces from her old adobe home in the Catalina foothills. Specializing in authentic furniture, old doors, window

Courtesy of Bahti Indian Arts

doors, *trasteros* (cupboards), and benches, Heidi also carries an assortment of trunks on stands, wardrobes, and coffee and dining tables made from old doors set on ox yoke bases. Many of the pieces have been painted and repainted in a variety of colors, and she restores the pieces through a careful sanding and waxing process that leaves just the right amount of color and texture to create a subtle, weathered effect.

All of the pieces at Tierra Madre are *hecho por mano* (hand-made), and most come from little mountain villages in Mexico. In addition to furniture, Heidi also carries fun accessories such as old sombreros, mesquite tortilla presses, and wonderful Talavera pottery that offers the flavor of old Mexico. Prices range from $25 (pottery) to $1400 (wardrobe).

Your trip to Tucson will likely feel somewhat incomplete if you miss the chance to get gussied up in cowboy or cowgirl duds. There are many Western-wear stores in Tucson, but the following are local favorites in which you can find one-of-kind and authentic attire. Tucsonans are fortunate that two of the country's premier boot makers are located right here in the Sonoran Desert.

Urbane Cowgirl

Address: 303 E. Congress St.

Phone: 520-882-2822

Located in historic downtown, the Urbane Cowgirl is the place to find Western fashions with a funky twist. This shop carries beautiful boots, belts, and skirts, and offers "elegance in fine Southwestern fashions."

Arizona Hatters

Address: 3600 N. First Ave., and 3800 E. Sunrise Ave.

Phone: First Ave. – 520-292-1320; Sunrise Ave. – 520-577-5812

Unlike many of the chain Western-wear stores, Arizona Hatters has been part of the Tucson community for more than 30 years, outfitting Tucsonans with the best in custom shaped and sized cowboy hats. In addition, Arizona Hatters offers the unique service of providing a stagecoach and a supply of custom hats for any parties or meetings you may have planned.

Corral Western Wear

Address: 4525 E. Broadway Blvd.

Phone: 520-322-6001

Corral has apparel for the entire family including clothing by Levi and Wrangler, and great boots by Stewart, Tony Lama, and Justin. This roomy store carries the latest Western wear, as well as more traditional cowboy duds.

Courtesy of Stewart Boot

Stewart Boot Company

Address: 30 W. 28th St.

Phone: 520-791-9973

For over 50 years, Stewart has been providing custom boots for cowboys all over the world. Many agree that Stewart boots are the best handmade boots money can buy. You can visit their workshop and have your own custom boots made by driving a little south of downtown.

Bond Boot Company

Address: 915 W. Masonic Dr., Nogales, AZ

Phone: 520-281-0512

Former rodeo star Paul Bond has made custom boots for the likes of Johnny Cash and John Wayne, and he continues his craft today in his shop in Nogales. You can choose from over 400 of Bond's designs, or design one of your own.

Outdoor Gear

Whether you forgot your hiking boots, or you need a new backpack, both of these stores will help you out. It would be a shame to visit the Old Pueblo without venturing into the beautiful mountains, desert, and other external arenas, and these stores carry all you need to enjoy your outdoor experience to its fullest extent.

Summit Hut

Address: 5045 E. Speedway Blvd.

Phone: 520-325-1554

Summit Hut has been Tucson's favorite provider of high-quality outdoor gear and clothing for years. If you're in the market for new sunglasses, hiking boots, or outdoor guidebooks, Summit Hut is the place to find them. And, if you need to rent equipment for your adventures, the Summit Hut has a full selection of camping gear to meet your needs. The Speedway location is the biggest and most comprehensive. The sales staff at each store is extremely knowledgeable about their equipment as well as about great local areas to visit.

Bob's Bargain Barn

Address: 2230 N. Country Club Rd.

Phone: 520-325-3409

Bob's Bargain Barn has been offering equipment for outdoor camping, hiking, fishing, and mountain gear for getting around Tucson's outback for more than 40 years. It has developed a reputation – among locals and visitors alike – for nearly always having the equipment you want, and offering it at a reasonable price.

Bookstores

Tucson has more than 50 bookstores, many of which specialize in one or several types of books. Today, the number of used bookstores is as great as the number of specialty book shops in the Southwest. The following is a listing of unique stores – we've left out the mall chain stores so that your visits to bookstores in Tucson will be different from the ones in your hometown.

Booked Up

Address: 2828 N. Stone Ave.

Phone: 520-622-8238

Booked Up is Tucson's choice for used and rare books on all subjects. They also feature antiques, artifacts, and *objets d'art*. This fascinating store is a great place to spend the afternoon browsing through one of the best, and most discriminating, collections of books in the city. They also have many interesting signed and first editions.

Antigone Books

Address: 411 N. Fourth Ave.

Phone: 520-792-3715

Antigone specializes in books by and about women. Their collection of books on women's studies and feminist theory is extensive. They also have a great children's section and a comprehensive collection of gay and lesbian literature.

Bookman's

Address: 1930 E. Grant Rd., and 3733 W. Ina Rd.

Phone: Grant Rd. 520-325-5767; Ina Rd. 520-579-0303

Bookman's is a Tucson tradition and Arizona's largest bookstore – the Grant Road location used to be a supermarket, so you can imagine the vast shelf space available. The store sells mostly used books, but it also features used CDs, maps, comics, and video games. The newsstand is huge, with new magazines, literary journals, and newspapers from all over the world. They also have a collectible section. Bookman's continues to expand its already-huge inventory, and it's possible to spend four or five hours browsing through the stores. To begin your exploration, grab a map of the store as you walk in.

The Book Mark

Address: 5001 E. Speedway Blvd.

Phone: 520-881-6350

The Book Mark is a good general bookstore with an inventory of more than 200,000 books. The staff is especially helpful with special orders and book locating. They have extensive gardening, children's, and philosophy sections, as well as a good selection of large-print books. The Book Mark has been locally owned and operated since 1958, and is one of Tucson's most established bookstores.

Coyote's Voice Books

Address: Broadway Village Center, 16 S. Eastbourne Ave.

Phone: 520-327-6560

Located in Tucson's oldest shopping center, this is a small, but amazingly stocked, store. The owners are discriminating; you won't find cheesy romance novels, but you will find the best in contemporary fiction. Their selection of cooking, travel, and architecture books is among the best in Tucson – and better than most of the larger stores'. The shop's children's section is unique in that it contains many Spanish-English bilingual books and volumes about the West. They also have extensive sections of Native American, Chicano, and Latino literature. Recently, the store has begun carrying music, specifically Southern blues and jazz. Their collection of books on jazz and blues is probably the most comprehensive in Tucson. Recent book signings at Coyote's Voice have included Ana Castillo, Luis Alberto Urrea, and Charles Bowden.

The Haunted Bookshop

Address: 7211 N. Northern Ave.

Phone: 520-297-4843

The Haunted Bookshop has one of the best collections of contemporary fiction in Tucson. Their children's section is huge as well, and there's a tunnel for the kids to crawl through. Because it's located right next to Tohono Chul Park, the Haunted Bookshop is popular with both tourists and locals. It's a big store: 80,000-100,000 volumes. Recent book signings have included Martin Hewlett, Susan Lowell, Tony Hillerman, and Barbara Kingsolver. The store is now in its 20th year, and is a well-established part of Tucson's ever-growing literary scene. The store specializes in handling custom orders and sells no magazines.

Footprints of a Gigantic Hound

Address: Broadway Village Center, 123 S. Eastbourne Ave.

Phone: 520-326-8533

This mystery bookstore takes its name from Sherlock Holmes's *The Hounds of Baskerville* and is complete with its own hound – a giant Irish Wolf Hound who lounges behind the counter. Footprints is Tucson's only mystery bookstore, and its selection – comprised of more than 5,000 volumes – is quite comprehensive. Recent signings have included Sue Grafton, Marcia Muller, Ross Thomas, and Tony Hillerman.

Books West Southwest

Address: 2452 N. Campbell Ave.

Phone: 520-326-3533

At Books West Southwest, the emphasis is on books about the American West, of course. They have good selections of Native American fiction and non-fiction, history, nature, art, cookbooks, guidebooks, and children's literature.

Whatever your taste in music, you don't have to look far find something to suit you. On any given afternoon, hundreds of Tucsonans are out flipping through bins of shiny new CDs or classic used vinyl in Tucson's many record stores. These are a few of the best...

Zia Record Exchange

Address: 3655 N. Oracle Rd.; and 7191 E. Speedway Blvd.

Phone: Oracle Rd. – 520-887-6898;
E. Speedway Blvd. – 520-290-2443

Zia is a welcome import from Phoenix, and has become a favorite source of music for Tucsonans since it arrived a few years ago. They offer a wide selection of new and used CDs in all musical categories, especially alternative and rock. They also sell t-shirts and books.

PDQ Records and Tapes

Address: 2342 N. Dodge Blvd.

Phone: 520-881-2681

PDQ is one of the last places that carries an extensive stock of vinyl records. Their CD selection, both new and used, is also quite large, and they specialize in imports.

Jeff's Classical Records

Address: 2556 N. Campbell Ave.

Phone: 520-327-0555

Jeff's is Tucson's primary source for classical records, CDs, and cassettes. They specialize in imports, movie soundtracks, and collector's items.

Tucson has more than 50 antique and collectible stores; some are fly-by-night, most others are established and reputable. Popular now are antique malls, where many dealers are located under one roof. There is a friendly network of shops in Tucson, and if one store doesn't have what you're looking for, they will usually set you in the right direction. Listed below is just a sampling of the shops around town.

The Antique Mall

Address: 3130 E. Grant Rd.

Phone: 520-326-3070

With over 60 dealers, The Antique Mall has everything from rare books to dinette sets. The spacious mall is also good for kitchen and country collectibles, glassware, and jewelry.

Firehouse Antiques Center

Address: 6522 E. 22nd St.

Phone: 520-571-1775

Although it's not as big as the Antique Mall or Unique Antique, Firehouse's multi-dealer inventory is quite impressive. They have everything from roll-top desks to Bionic Woman dolls.

Gertrude's Collectibles

Address: 118 E. Congress St.

Phone: 520-884-5912

Gertrude's is packed with newer collectible toys, glassware and curios. The store's primary emphasis is on action figures, and its walls are adorned with hundreds of these mighty men, women, and monsters, from Star Wars to Teenage Mutant Ninja Turtles.

Saguaro Moon Antiques

Address: 45 S. Sixth Ave.

Phone: 520-623-5393

This store has tons of kitchenware, appliances, magazines, and toys from the '50s and '60s. They also have jukeboxes, clocks, and many Western goods.

Unique Antique

Address: 5000 E. Speedway Blvd.

Phone: 520-323-0319

Ninety dealers have set up shop in Unique Antique, the antique outlet voted to be the best by readers of the *Tucson Weekly.* Like most antique malls, Unique Antique has everything. It is especially rich in kitsch, toys, and housewares.

Thrift Stores

Designer Todd Oldham says shopping at thrift stores is like "digging in someone's purse, but it's better because you don't get in trouble."

Designer Todd Oldham says shopping at thrift stores is like "digging in someone's purse, but it's better because you don't get in trouble." According to the same article in *Vogue,* Tucson is one of Oldham's favorite haunts for thrift store shopping. With the plethora of thrift stores in Tucson – many of which are near each other – it's easy to see why…

The following are actual thrift stores, not stores full of items bought at other thrift stores. At these stores, you can still buy a jacket for under $3, and dishes for 30¢ each. All of these rely on donations and benefit charities.

Assistance League Thrift & Craft Shop

Address: 1307 N. Alvernon Way

Phone: 520-326-1585

The most impressive aspect of this store is its cleanliness. All items are clearly marked with prices and the store is highly staffed with volunteers. The inventory does change, but not as quickly as it does in some of the bigger thrift stores. Best bets here are vintage clothes, toys, and books. Best Finds: First Edition *Slaughterhouse-five* for $1, Six Million Dollar Man board game for $2, Disco motif cocktail glass for 50¢.

Casa de los Niños Thrift Superstore

Address: 1302 E. Prince Rd.

Phone: 520-325-2573

One of Tucson's biggest thrift stores (the building used to be a supermarket), this shop's inventory is huge and highly mercurial. By far, your best bets are in the toy department. There are hundreds of action figures – some old – Barbies and board games. It's also a good place to find children's clothing and kitchen appliances. Best Finds: '70s Ken doll with fetching leisure suit for $3, '60s toaster for $4, beautifully weathered cowboy boots for $9.

Speedway Outlet

Address: 5421 E. Speedway Blvd.

Phone: 520-323-7760

Speedway Outlet is gigantic, and has an ever-changing inventory. Prices here are slightly higher than you'll find at other thrift stores, but there's usually better stuff. The clothes are good: wool flannel shirts, Levis, combat boots. There's a collectible section which contains items that seem to be somewhat randomly priced. Good toy and houseware sections. Best Finds: Suede coat for $16, wool flannel shirts for $5, Happy Days puzzle for $1.

Value Village

Address: 300 N. Fourth Ave.

Phone: 520-624-3414

There's always something good at Value Village and it's usually quite cheap. If you spend ten minutes in the store, you'll find something you want to take home. Value Village is best for tacky gimcracks, toys, clothes – everything. Pricing seems random, but it's almost always to the customer's advantage. This place is huge, and has prosthetic arms and legs hanging from the ceiling alongside fur coats and shawls. Best Finds: Chewbacca Star Wars figure for 10¢, Army Surplus Parka for $2, Charlie's Angels lunch box for $2, hardback *Ciderhouse Rules* for $1, Bermuda shorts for 60¢.

Tucson is also a hub for great "vintage" boutiques. Most are on Fourth Avenue, making it easy to visit many in just a few hours or minutes. While the prices are higher than at the above thrift stores that benefit charities, all the merchandise is still cheap – much cheaper than in similar stores in L.A. and New York.

Buffalo Exchange

Address: 2001 E. Speedway Blvd.; 7045 E. Tanque Verde Rd.; 1702 E. Prince Rd.

Phone: E. Speedway Blvd. – 520-795-0508; E. Tanque Verde Rd. – 520-885-8392; E. Prince Rd. – 520-881-8438

Tucson was the home of the first Buffalo Exchange back in 1974, and now the company has grown to include stores in San Francisco, San Diego, and Albuquerque. They buy 85% of their inventory from the public, and they're discriminating, so the store is packed with only good stuff. They have current styles for both women and men, vintage and new. The inventory changes every minute, as they are constantly buying more clothing. The main Buffalo Exchange is located on Speedway Blvd. near the university, and another Buffalo Exchange specializing in women's career clothing is located on the far east side of town on Tanque Verde Road. There is also a store devoted to children's clothing appropriately named "Buffalo Kids" which is centrally located on E. Prince Road.

Desert Vintage and Costume

Address: 636 N. Fourth Ave.

Phone: 520-620-1570

This little boutique specializes in apparel from the 1920s to the 1960s – "Victoriola to Psychedelia." Its selection of clothing can vary according to season and demand; for instance, Hawaiian shirts become available in the summer months. They also rent out costumes as well.

113

How Sweet it Was

Address: 531 N. Fourth Ave.

Phone: 520-623-9854

You can buy clothing from the 1800s at How Sweet it Was. They also carry apparel as new as from the '60s. Like a few other shops, they do costuming. Look for the mannequins on the sidewalk in front of the store.

Tucson Thrift

Address: 319 N. Fourth Ave.

Phone: 520-623-8736

This is a great place to find housewares, collectibles, and vintage clothing. They have a good selection of nicely worn Levis and military surplus-wear. Strange knickknacks also seem to be a specialty.

Miscellaneous

The cactus nurseries and the following three stores didn't fit into any category, but they shouldn't be missed.

Tanque Verde Greenhouses

Address: 10810 E. Tanque Verde Rd.

Phone: 520-749-4414

Hours: M-Sat 9 a.m. to 5 p.m.

When people visit greenhouses, they often expect to find lush, exotic plants whose true homes are somewhere in the tropical regions of the world. Most don't expect to see cacti, and many may think of this arid desert plant as being rather dry and uninteresting. Then again, most people haven't been to the Tanque Verde Greenhouses. Featuring such cacti as the Mammillaria from Mexico, or the Lobivia species from South America, the Tanque Verde Greenhouses offer proof enough that these strange plants are nothing short of astonishing. Witness the brilliant colors the flowers exude during the early part of the year, and you may find yourself walking out with more than just this guidebook in hand.

Open since 1964, Tanque Verde Greenhouses is a large supplier of cactus to individuals and the wholesalers alike. With more than 500 species and a million plants in stock, they specialize in flowering cacti, which they have collected from all over the world. With a knowledgeable and friendly staff on hand to answer any questions you may have with regards to these unusual plants, you will feel more like you're in an arboretum or botanical garden than in a commercial greenhouse.

Should you choose to buy a plant, or one of their popular ready-to-go dish gardens, you needn't worry about travel damage, as they will carefully package your plants for the trip home. If you prefer, they'll also ship your selected cacti anywhere in the United States.

B & B Cactus Farm

Address: 11550 E. Speedway Blvd.

Phone: 520-721-4687

Hours: M-Sat, 9 a.m. to 5 p.m., open Sundays November-April (call for hours).

This cactus nursery has many greenhouses that are open to the public for viewing and making purchases. B & B also offers a range of other succulents that might just be the perfect companion plant for that cactus you have at home. Like Tanque Verde, they will ship anywhere in the U.S., and B & B Cactus Farm has a small selection of books about the Southwest and Tucson that you may find interesting.

Tucson's Map and Flag Center

Address: 3239 N. First Ave.

Phone: 520-887-4234

The Center offers the largest selection of maps and flags in Southern Arizona, as well as a wide selection of books on the Southwest. Their maps represent the entire world – in fact, you may find a better map of your own home town at the Center than you could find in a store back home. It also carries great books and maps for tourists interested in exploring parts of Arizona that are usually known only by natives, such as ghost towns, ruins, and less populated hikes.

Discount Agate House

Address: 3401 N. Dodge Blvd.

Phone: 520-323-0781

The Agate House carries minerals from around the world. Recently, they were voted by *Tucson Weekly* as being the best place to buy cheap souvenirs, such as polished, exotic-looking rocks for 25¢.

Sonoran Desert Marketplace

Address: 1333 N. Oracle Rd.

Phone: 520-624-4018

In addition to being a mineral retailer, the Sonoran Desert Marketplace carries Tucson's largest selection of fossils. Located in a 60-year-old building that is a blend of Art Deco and Pueblo architecture, it also offers Native American arts and crafts and local foods.

To help you make the most of your shopping time in Tucson, we've compiled the following maps of stores that are within close proximity of one another in different areas of town.

Congress Street/Downtown

❶ *Berta Wright*

❷ *Picante / Yikes*

❸ *Old Town Artisans*

❹ *Tucson Museum of Art Gift Shop*

❺ *Urbane Cowgirl*

❻ *Gertrude's Collectibles*

❼ *Saguaro Moon*

Fourth Avenue

❶ *Antigone Books*

❷ *Value Village*

❸ *How Sweet it Was*

❹ *Desert Vintage and Costume*

❺ *Tucson Thrift*

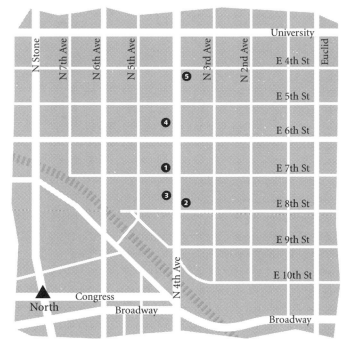

Campbell Avenue

❶ *Kaibab Shops*

❷ *Bookman's*

❸ *Books West Southwest*

❹ *Jeff's Classical Records*

The nightlife in Tucson has picked up dramatically over the last five years or so. On any given weekend night, the streets of downtown are quite crowded with club hoppers and patrons of the arts, even during the hot summer months. The night scene is as culturally diverse and eclectic as the city itself. For information on events taking place in Tucson, pick up the latest copy of Tucson Weekly, an arts and entertainment newspaper which is available for free all over the city. You can also check out the Friday edition of the Arizona Daily Star, which has a special pull-out section entitled "Starlight," or the "Calendar" section in the Thursday edition of the Tucson Citizen, both of which feature upcoming events.

Every first and third Saturday night of the month, Tucson's downtown area comes alive with musicians, street performers, and vendors hawking the latest in everything from jewelry to books on Buddhism. The many galleries, specialty shops, and restaurants in the area remain open into the evening. This bi-weekly event is Downtown Saturday Night, which is put on by the Tucson Arts District Partnership, Inc. (520-624-9977) to celebrate Tucson's eclectic and multi-faceted culture.

With much of the action centered around Congress Street, performances can occur anywhere from the Ronstadt Center, to Broadway Boulevard, and down into Arizona Alley. Recent performances have been given by the Tucson Symphony Ensemble, a pair of comical pirates shouting Shakespearean orations, various dance groups, and a host of musicians playing everything from country, folk, and blues, to rock and jazz.

Also adding to the action is the Fourth Avenue Merchants Association (520-624-5004), which has been promoting a similar and simultaneous celebration on Downtown Saturday Nights along the Fourth Avenue corridor.

Tucson has more than its share of bars and nightclubs, so we've chosen to include a few that best represent the Tucson lifestyle.

The Shelter

Address: 4155 E. Grant Rd.

Phone: 520-326-1345

The Shelter, Tucson's favorite dive, is decorated in kitsch and frequented by all walks of life. It's an authentic '60s cocktail lounge – with a wacky staff – that plays everything from easy-listening music to contemporary jazz, soul, and R&B. If you're lucky, you'll catch Maebelle, the wife of the club's owner, on an evening when she performs her original singing act. The selection of beer is broad, and includes a large number of imports and microbrewed labels.

The Bum Steer

Address: 1910 N. Stone Ave.

Phone: 520-884-7377

The Bum Steer always has food and drink specials. You can spend hours gazing at the junk hanging up in the ceiling. This place is huge, with sand volleyball courts in the back, and is a great place for burgers and beer. Kids are welcome during meal times, too.

Club Congress

Address: 311 E. Congress St.

Phone: 520-622-8849

There's always something happening at Club Congress, located on the first floor of the historic Congress Hotel in downtown Tucson. They host local musicians as well as big-name performers such as Jonathan Richman and the Meat Puppets. Most of the acts are alternative or folk. When there's no live music, Congress promotes theme nights that feature disco, techno, or other music styles. The Tap Room, a tiny bar on the north side of the building, offers drink specials. There's also a small cafe with an extensive menu. This is a great place to get a sense of the Tucson scene, and every visitor should spend an evening at Congress. Call them for event information, and choose your night.

Gentle Ben's Brewing Company

Address: 865 E. University Ave.

Phone: 520-624-4177

Gentle Ben's is Tucson's only microbrewery. With 15,000 square feet spanning two floors, and a capacity of 900 people, the club also serves as a popular live music venue. Usually the acts on stage are local performers, and its a good idea to call ahead for details on who's playing. The wide patio that overlooks the university campus is perfect for enjoying spring and fall evenings, and is a great place for people of all ages to gather. Gentle Ben's is scheduled to open in its new location in January 1996.

Cushing Street Bar and Grill

Address: 343 S. Meyer Ave.

Phone: 520-622-7984

Cushing Street has been providing Tucson with music for years. With nightly acts that include blues, rock, and folk music played by talented local and out-of-town musicians, Cushing Street is an intimate, unpretentious club that's ideal for serious fans of music. It's located in the beautifully preserved Barrio Historico neighborhood, in a building that's 100 years old.

Berky's

Address: 5769 E. Speedway Blvd., and 424 N. Fourth Ave.

Phone: E. Speedway Blvd. – 520-296-1981,
N. Fourth Ave. – 520-622-0376

Berky's offers live music six nights per week, mostly R & B, Motown, and pure blues. While the atmosphere here is not exactly refined, the clientele is sophisticated both in musical matters and other aspects. Call them for a schedule of performances.

Café Sweetwater

Address: 340 E. 6th St.
Phone: 520-622-6464

Café Sweetwater is one of Tucson's only establishments in which the primary focus is on jazz music. It's here that you'll find most of the more prominent jazz musicians in the area, as they jam in the evenings on Thursday through Saturday. On occasion, renowned entertainers have been known to take the stage. This is a great place to go with a date or a friend, as it's quiet enough to hold a conversation, and if you're so inclined, you can also take advantage of the club's dance floor. There's also a good restaurant on the premises that has a varied menu.

Refer to page131 for information on the Tucson Jazz Society.

Honky Tonks and Western Clubs

Maverick, King of Clubs

Address: 4702 E. 22nd St.
Phone: 520-748-0456

The Maverick has been a honky-tonking Tucson tradition for over 30 years. It's an unassuming place that lacks the flash of some of the newer clubs. They offer two-step and line-dancing lessons for neophytes to the world of country music. The staff is friendly, the clientele non-pretentious. The club often hosts two bands per night, and there's sometimes a cover for special events.

Cactus Moon

Address: 5470 E. Broadway Blvd.
Phone: 520-748-0049

One of the newest Western dance clubs, the Cactus Moon is high-tech with a dance floor that is as well-suited for John Travolta hustling to the Bee Gees as it is for cowboys two-stepping to Randy Travis. Different drink specials and cover charges exist throughout the week. Call for details.

A Little Bit of Texas

Address: 4385 W. Ina Rd.

Phone: 520-744-7744

A Little Bit of Texas, formally named the Wild Wild West, is known for Two Steppin and Long Neckin. Not only are there dance floors and bars, but there are places to buy new boots and giant belt buckles. You can even dress up like a pioneer and have your picture taken. All of this is under one roof – with drink specials to boot.

CCC Chuckwagon Suppers

Address: 8900 Bopp Rd.

Phone: 520-883-2333, 1-800-446-1798

For a great night of steaks and traditional Western music, drive out to Bopp Road, where the admission price to CCC Chuckwagon includes dinner and a show. A fun place for the entire family, this entertaining music and dining venue opens for the winter season in late December. There's a Western gift shop on the premises. You must call for reservations.

Casinos

While Tucson is no Las Vegas, it will suffice for those looking for a night or two of gambling. In addition to the many bingo halls, Tucson has two casinos.

25 miles west of Tucson is the Tohono O'odham Reservation which covers about 2,800,000 acres. It is the second largest reservation in the country.

Desert Diamond Casino

Address: 7350 Old Nogales Highway

Phone: 520-889-7354

The Desert Diamond Casino, located 15 minutes from downtown, is home to hundreds of quarter and dollar slot machines, a large bingo facility, and countless video blackjack, craps, poker, and keno machines. Proceeds from Desert Diamond benefit the Tohono O'Odham Nation by directly providing funds and by creating employment opportunities for Native American and non-Indian people in the area.

Casino of the Sun

Address: 7406 S. Camino de Oeste

Phone: 520-883-1700

The Casino of the Sun is farther from downtown Tucson than Desert Diamond but, in addition to the 500 slot (some nickel) and video machines, it offers live-action cards, a non-smoking area, and million dollar bingo. The Casino of the Sun benefits the Pascua Yaqui Tribe.

Family Fun

There's no need to leave the kids in the hotel when you go out, as Tucson has something for everyone. If you're looking for some family fun, you'll find plenty of bowling, skating, mini-golf and other family-style opportunities in the area. Here are just a few...

Fiesta Lanes

Address: 501 W. River Rd.

Phone: 520-887-2695

In addition to providing full bowling facilities, Fiesta Lanes also has a game room with pool and pinball games, and a snack bar.

Golden Pin Lanes

Address: 1010 W. Miracle Mile

Phone: 520-888-4272

Golden Pin's full-service bowling center is the home of the Pro Bowlers tour. They have a full cocktail lounge, bumper and colored pin bowling for the kids, as well as an entertaining game room and a coffee shop filled with snacks.

Lucky Strike Bowl

Address: 4015 E. Speedway Blvd.

Phone: 520-327-4926

This traditional bowling center is located just 15 minutes east of downtown. The Lucky Strike is a Tucson institution, and has long been favored by locals.

Skate Country: East and North

Address: East – 7980 E. 22nd St., North – 2700 N. Stone Ave.

Phone: East – 520-298-4409; North – 520-622-6650

Tucson still has two fully-operational roller-rinks that date back to the days when satin shorts and Donna Summer were all the rage. Disco lights and cheesy murals at both locations give even the most discriminating roller-disco enthusiasts an authentic flashback to 1980. Don't fret if you're just looking for exercise and you hate pulsating disco music, you'll find what you're looking for at the Skate Countries. The DJs most often play country-western or rock music, and keep the strobe lights turned low.

Rental skates are available at both Skate Country locations. North offers traditional roller-skates while East rents both traditional and in-line skates. Each location is equipped with a pro-shop, a snack bar, and entertaining arcade games to round out your skating experience. Because some skating specials are not suitable for children, we recommend that you call ahead if you're planning to bring the little ones.

Golf N' Stuff

Address: 6503 E. Tanque Verde Rd.

Phone: 520-296-2366

Golf N' Stuff offers miniature golf, bumper boats, an extensive arcade, bumper cars, batting cages, a snack bar, and Lit'l Indy race cars. All of this adds up to some serious fun for kids and parents alike!

Funtasticks Family Fun Park

Address: 221 E. Wetmore Rd.

Phone: 520-888-GOLF (4653)

Funtasticks, conveniently located near the Tucson Mall, offers something for everyone: go-karts, a kiddie roller coaster, two 18-hole mini-golf courses, bumper boats, batting cages, a large video game area, and a food court with a pizzeria.

Discovery Zone Fun Center

6238 E. Broadway Blvd.

520-748-9190

Discovery Zone prides itself on being "the ultimate indoor playground" for kids 12 and under. It lives up to its nickname with roller slides, waterbed walks, obstacle courses, and ball rooms. It's a safe place where kids can go wild, and there's even a special section for kids under 40 inches tall. A full eatery is on the premises, too.

The Performing Arts

Tucson is one of only 14 cities in the United States with symphony, theater, ballet, and opera companies, and was recently cited as a "mini-mecca" for the arts by theWall Street Journal.

Theater

Tucson has many offerings for theater lovers. Call or check the local newspapers for schedules and tickets prices for current productions.

a.k.a. Theater Company

Address: 125 E. Congress St.

Phone: 520-623-7852

Tickets for this tiny theater usually cost about ten dollars, with discounts for seniors, students, and artists. Performing in the 50-seat auditorium, artists in this semi-professional company specialize in original and experimental productions. Recent plays produced here include, *Ubu Cocu*, Alfred Jarry's sequel to his *Ubu Roi*, and Y. York's *Rain, Some Fish, No Elephants*.

Arizona Children's Theatre Company

Address: *El Con Mall, 3601 E. Broadway Blvd.*

Phone: *520-795-9314*

In the eight years since the Arizona Children's Theatre Company was founded in El Con Mall, the company has presented outstanding productions of the world's fairy tales, folk stories, and improvisational narratives to more than 20,000 people. Recent productions include *Rumplestiltskin*, and other stories that promote the revival of our nearly extinct "oral tradition."

Arizona Rose Theatre Company

Address: *TCC Leo Rich Theatre, 260 S. Church Ave.*

Phone: *520-791-4836*

Now in its eighth year, the Rose Theatre was originally established as a venue for light-hearted performances that incorporate comedy and music to share humor and positive ideas. The company draws largely on local talent – with casts both large and small – to perform such musicals as the humorous *Push Play for Murder* and *Rainbow Country Fair*.

Tucson is one of only 14 cities in the United States that has a resident symphony, theater, ballet and opera companies. Tucson was recently cited as a "mini-mecca" for the arts by The Wall Street Journal.

Arizona Theatre Company

Address: *Temple of Music and Art, 330 S. Scott Ave.*

Phone: *520-622-2823*

The only resident professional theater company in Arizona, the Arizona Theatre Company produces a wide variety of work, ranging from contemporary to classical. Unique in that it performs in two cities, this regional company has recently executed exceptional performances of Michael Frayn's *Noises Off*, and *A Midsummer Night's Dream*, courtesy of Sir William Shakespeare.

Gaslight Theatre

Address: *7010 E. Broadway Blvd.*

Phone: *520-886-9428*

Seats at Gaslight performances are sometimes hard to come by, as many of its family-oriented shows are sold out well in advance. Pizza, popcorn, and beverages help keep the hunger away, as you take in such popular productions as

Sinbad, A Christmas Carol, and *The Phantom of the Opera,* which was skillfully adapted by Peter Van Slyke. The Gaslight has scheduled performances year-round, so call for their current offerings.

Invisible Theatre

Address: 1400 N. First Ave.

Phone: 520-882-9721

Established more than 23 years ago, the Invisible Theater is another well-loved Tucson tradition. The theater has seating for eighty and a takes its name from the invisible energy that's believed to build between the performers and their audiences to produce the magic of theater. While this theater originally presented exclusively local work, their seasons now include one featured musical annually, plus some classical and contemporary plays. They have performed plays such as *The Real Inspector Hound,* a British comedy, and the bilingual *Carreño.*

Southern Arizona Light Opera Company (SALOC)

Address: TCC Music Hall, 908 N. Swan (box office)

Phone: 520-323-7888 or 520-884-1212

Having produced more than 70 shows in its history, this musical theater is today one of Arizona's largest organizations of the performing arts. SALOC draws audiences from throughout Southern Arizona for such top-quality performances as *Guys and Dolls, A Chorus Line, Peter Pan,* and *Cinderella.* As there is almost always a popular production on the boards at this theater, it's well worth the effort to check the current schedule.

UA Theatre Arts/Arizona Repertory Theatre

Address: The Fine Arts Complex, University of Arizona Campus

Phone: 520-621-1162

You'll also want to see what the U of A has to offer for theater lovers. Dedicated to producing plays that investigate the human condition and other timeless issues, the Arizona Repertory Theatre produces classical European and American work, contemporary pieces, and inspiring musicals. Recent performances have included *The Importance of Being Earnest, A Tale of Two Cities,* and *Lend Me a Tenor.*

The dance scene in Tucson is lively, and includes everything from outstanding traditional ballet to contemporary modern dance. Special series also breeze through town – from Broadway to the Bolshoi – and Tucson welcomes dance luminaries from around the world.

Ballet Arizona

Address: *Tucson Convention Center Music Hall, 260 S. Church Ave. (unless noted)*

Phone: *520-822-5022*

This international troupe is based in Phoenix, and is the state's official ballet company. Dancers are natives of many countries: China, Columbia, Japan, and Switzerland, to name a few. Ballet Arizona not only performs traditional ballets, but also more contemporary ones such as the radical version of *Alice in Wonderland* that includes music from Bach and The Red Hot Chili Peppers. Most recently, the company performed the exquisite *Carmina Burana*.

Orts Theatre of Dance

Address: *Performances are presented in various locations.*

Phone: *520-624-3799*

If you're lucky enough to be in town during an Orts performance, make sure you catch it. This modern dance troupe is

A modern dance performance by the Orts Theatre of Dance.

one of Tucson's largest and longest running companies, and will stun you with its innovative movements and interpretations. Performances include contemporary work by celebrated choreographers from around the world.

Southwest Dance

Address: Performances are presented in various locations.

Phone: 602-482-6410

Southwest Dance imports terrific troupes from all over the world to perform in Tucson. Dedicated to presenting "world class" dance to audiences in Arizona – the desired result being a wider recognition of this inimitable art form – this organization plans to expand its efforts throughout the Southwest in the future. Distinguished international dance companies from Chicago, Venezuela, Winnipeg, and Hong Kong are among the troupes that have recently entertained and inspired Tucson audiences.

Music

Tucson has its own symphony and opera company, and it hosts various performers from all over the globe. Whether you're into classical opera, contemporary and traditional jazz, the transcendent experience offered by a full orchestra, or anything in between, you're sure to find something to suit your musical tastes in Tucson.

Arizona Friends of Chamber Music

Address: Tucson Convention Center, Leo Rich Theatre, 260 S. Church Ave.

Phone: 520-298-5806

This venerable organization has been entertaining Tucson audiences for more than 48 years by bringing world-class performers from as far away as Tokyo and featuring exceptional local talent. Arizona Friends presents seven shows in its talent-packed season, all of which are truly memorable events.

Arizona Opera

Address: Tucson Convention Center Music Hall, 260 S. Church Ave.

Phone: 520-293-4336

Tucson's opera company has performed such operatic classics as *Carmen* and *Götterdämmerung*. Established in 1972, this state-wide company stages five productions per year, each of which features internationally acclaimed conductors and performers. Call for information on tickets for specific shows.

Tucson Symphony Orchestra

Address: Performs in various venues.

Phone: 520-882-8585

Established in 1929, this highly respected orchestra is the oldest in the Southwest, and is home to some of the world's finest musicians. Classic Concerts, Pops Parade, Chamber Concerts, and Recitals are among the season's offerings, and several special concerts are held throughout the year. Recent guests of the Tucson Symphony Orchestra have been Cho-Liang Lin, who soloed Brahms, *Violin Concerto*, and Anthony Newman, the outlandish American organist.

University of Arizona UA Presents

Address: Centennial Hall, University of Arizona Campus

Phone: 520-621-3341

The UA Presents Series for classical music has brought in such big names as Marilyn Horne and Christopher Parkening, and continues to summon distinguished artists for the enjoyment of those who appreciate classical music.

The Tucson Jazz Society

Address: P.O. Box 85101, Tucson, AZ 85754

Phone: 520-743-3399

Tucson is a favorable environment for jazz aficionados of all sorts, especially since the founding of this organization 18 years ago. The Tucson Jazz Society is dedicated to promoting the appreciation of this diverse musical style, and presents a jazz series in the spring and in the fall, with a big band series in the winter months. Primavera is the country's oldest women's jazz event, and the Plaza Suite Series showcases both local and national groups. For up-to-the-minute information on the area jazz scene, call the Society's Jazz Hotline at 520-743-3399.

Tucson is virtually overflowing with culture and art. Those who enjoy contemplating or purchasing fine art will be glad to discover the many fine galleries for which Tucson is known.

If you are in town on a Thursday, you can attend the Thursday Night ArtWalk that's sponsored by the Tucson Arts District Partnership (520-624-9977). Except on Thanksgiving, galleries are open for the event from 5 p.m. to 7:30 p.m. You can pick up a map for the self-guided tour from one of the many galleries, museums, or art spaces that

Anna Franklin's wooden dolls.

participate in the ArtWalk, or obtain one by calling the Partnership at the above number. Many cafe and other shops also participate in the evening affair.

Below you'll find just a small sampling of Tucson's many galleries. For a more extensive listing, pick up a copy of *Art Life*, available free at most galleries and studios.

Anna Franklin – Dolls and Marionettes

Address: 825 N. Anita (Barrio Anita)

Phone: 520-792-0777

Hours: By appointment only

Anna's beautiful dolls and marionettes are carved from redwood, hand painted, then dressed in colorful, hand-sewn costumes and detailed with jewelry, beadwork, and ribbons. These unique dolls and marionettes are true folk art figures that portray a likeness to the indigenous peoples of North and Central America.

De Grazia Art and Cultural Foundation

See the listing for the De Grazia Gallery in the Sun in the Attractions section of this book.

El Presidio Gallery

Address: Santa Fe Square, 7000 Tanque Verde Rd.,
St. Philip's Plaza, 4340 N. Campbell

Phone: Santa Fe Square – 520-733-0388, St. Philip's Plaza –
520-529-1220

Hours: M-Sat from 10 a.m. to 5 p.m.

The El Presidio is one of the larger galleries in town, and sells many fine pieces of Southwestern art, ceramics, and bronze work. Both locations carry paintings by Sue Krzyston, Lawrence W. Lee, and Mary E. Wyant, as well as works by other notable artists. If you like bronze art, you will probably enjoy the detail of the Western and Southwestern-style bronzes by C. Ross Morgan.

Etherton Gallery

Address: 135 S. Sixth Ave.

Phone: 520-624-7370

Hours: Sept. through May, Tu-Sat 12 p.m. to 5 p.m.;
June through August, by appointment only.

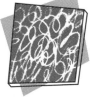

Considered one of the most distinguished galleries in the Southwest, the Etherton Gallery specializes in vintage and contemporary Western American ethnographic and landscape photographs. You will also find a great selection of contemporary paintings, sculptures, and prints. Recent showings have included works by Bailey Doogan, Holly Roberts, Randy Spalding, Charles Bayly, and Jeff Jonczyk.

Obsidian Gallery

Address: St. Philip's Plaza,
4340 N. Campbell

Phone: 520-577-3598

Hours: M-Sat 10 a.m. to 5:30 p.m.

Offering a selection of fine contemporary crafts, the Obsidian Gallery sells art in a variety of media, including glass, clay, wood, fiber, metal, art jewelry, and mixed media. Reflecting the unique charm of the Southwest, the works at the Obsidian Gallery have been crafted by both well-known and still-emerging artists from Tucson and abroad.

Philabaum Contemporary Art Glass

Address: 711 S. Sixth Ave.

Phone: 520-884-7404

Hours: Tu-Sat, 11 to 6 p.m.

This glass blowing studio and gallery operates its "hot shop" full-time, creating beautiful and stunning pieces of contemporary art in the form of vases, bowls, perfume bottles, and paperweights. The Philabaum also offers glass blowing demonstrations to the general public, but you'll need to call ahead for times and dates.

Murals

For thousands of years, murals have existed as bigger-than-life expressions of the history, hopes, and dreams of the community in which they are found. Often filled with symbols and caricatures, murals are like open books whose words are shaped using colors, forms, and light.

Tucson is fortunate to have many murals throughout its city limits. Muralists such as David Tineo, Antonio Pazos, Luis Gustavo Mena, and many others have added new dimensions and meaning to many of the walls in the area. The most prominent mural, and probably the easiest to visit while you're downtown, is located on the north-facing wall of the Tucson Museum of Art (see the listing under *Attractions* for more information on the museum). This mural, painted in 1992, is a collaborative effort between Tineo and Pazos, and is more like two murals melded into one. The right portion of the mural – done by Tineo – is entitled, *Nuestros Raíces Humanas,* while the left portion was painted by Antonio Pazos and is called, *Nuestra Futura.* It would be unfair to try and describe this intricate work of art in such a short space, except to say that the mural endeavors to reflect the past, present, and future of Chicanos. It is bright with color, and is impressive indeed.

As Tucson has more than 190 murals, it would be impossible to list them all here. You'll see many of these colorful paintings in your travels around town, and the following are a few of the more well-known – and easy-to-find – works.

Untitled, 1991.

Untitled, 1991

Artist: Martin Moreno with neighborhood youth

Address: La Pilita Youth Resource Center, 420 S. Main Ave.

Return of the Bird Tribes

Artist: Agnese Heston

Address: Antigone Bookstore, 411 N. Fourth Ave.

In the Valley

Artist: Gustavo Rocha

Address: Sweet Grass Indian Supplies, 450 N. Main Ave.

El Rio Belongs to the People, La Familia, Tlaloc

Artist: Antonio Pazos

Address: El Rio Neighborhood Center, 1390 W. Speedway Blvd.

Daisy Eyes #2

Artist: Jon Murdo Matheson

Address: 25 E. Congress St.

Day Trips

While the vast array of things to see and do in Tucson is enough to keep you busy for weeks, we recommend that you plan some time to hit the road to get a feel for the incredible diversity that characterizes Southeastern Arizona. In addition to the spectacular desert environment and attractions reminiscent of the Old West – such as Tombstone – you'll find other fascinating historical sites, great local wineries, erstwhile mining towns, forested mountain slopes, strange towering rock formations, and the beaches on the Sea of Cortez, all within a day's drive of the city. Natural wonders aside, there are also some wonderful shops, restaurants, and places to stay at these day trip destinations. So grab your road map, hop in the car, and go!

Day Trips from Tucson

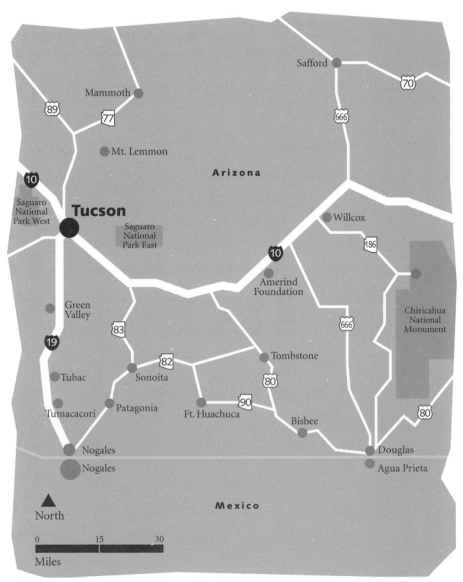

At time of printing, Highway 666 is being renumbered to Highway 191.

Tombstone

Directions: Take I-10 east to Benson, exit 303 and go through town and head south on Highway 80, approximately 65 miles southeast of Tucson.

Known as "The Town Too Tough to Die," Tombstone takes you back to the Old West like no other place. Located just 65 miles southeast of Tucson, Tombstone makes a perfect day trip or weekend getaway. The entire town is a Registered Historical Landmark, and when you see it, you'll understand why. It's hard to believe that the main strip of Tombstone is not a movie set, but a real town full of activity. Scanning the streets lined with late nineteenth century buildings, with purple mountains rising in the background, it's easy to let your imagination send you back in time.

While Tombstone may seem like a small town today, in the 1880s it was the largest community between San Francisco and St. Louis. It started as a small mining camp, but when word got around that the area was exceedingly rich in silver, Tombstone quickly exploded into a booming town. Many of the buildings that were built in that era are

Ladies in costume at Tombstone.

being used for the same purposes today. Schieffelin Hall was built in 1881 and still serves as a community entertainment hall, and Tombstone City Hall has served its purpose since its construction in 1882.

The Court House, which was used by Cochise County until 1929, is now a state park museum. It is located on Toughnut street between Third and Fourth Avenues. Exhibits include the cattlemen's room, the lawyers' room, and a room devoted entirely to antique costumes and household accessories. You may also want to peek at the hangman's platform before you leave the museum.

Tombstone is home to the famous O.K. Corral where it is still possible to witness a gunfight. It is located on Allen Street between Third and Fourth Avenues. While watching the action-packed show you will be occupying the same ground on which the Earp brothers and Doc Holliday once fought the Clanton and McLaury brothers.

Next door to the O.K. Corral on Allen Street is the Tombstone Historama. It offers an exciting multimedia presentation of "The Story of Tombstone." This is an informative show that provides a context to help you understand and appreciate the struggles of people who lived in this once-wild, and still-fascinating, silver mining town.

To get a sense of how you would have fared in this community a century ago, visit the Museum of the West at 109 S. Third Street. There, you can try to operate a 100-year-old washing machine or give the butter churn a whirl. You can also grind corn by hand, the traditional practice of Native American tribes. The museum has a few other oddities on display, including George Washington's desk, and even a lock of his hair.

Another Tombstone landmark is the Bird Cage Theatre. In 1882, the *New York Times* referred to it as, "The wildest, wickedest nightspot between Basin Street and the Barbary Coast." In fact, the theater hosted several cancan dancers and was a favorite hangout for many an outlaw and cowboy. Wyatt Earp met his third wife, Sadie Marcus, at the Bird Cage. The theater was also host to the West's longest poker game in history. It went on for eight years, five months, and three days. The theater got its name for the 14 bird cage crib compartments – still suspended from the ceiling – in which "ladies of the night" practiced their trade. The wall behind the bar is riddled with six bullet holes that bored right through the original bar painting of Fatima long ago. The authentic dumbwaiter that once sent drinks up to the courtesans' cages is also still intact. The Bird Cage Theatre is open daily and is located on Allen Street, east of Fifth Avenue.

The Crystal Palace Saloon is a good place to stop for a drink while visiting Tombstone. This saloon was home to the more refined crowd of Tombstone and did not cater to the crazy drunks that hung out at the Bird Cage. Its interior is more luxurious and the music is relaxing, making it a nice place to enjoy some food and drink.

If you want to buy, or just window shop for, Native American or local art, there are a few stores in town that have a nice variety from which to choose. Arlene's Gallery at 415 Allen Street has a great selection of Southwestern art, including sculpture, jewelry, and paintings. The Territorial Room, at the corner of Third and Allen, carries paintings, sculpture, pottery, stained glass, jewelry, prints, and works in leather and stone done by local artists. The Hon Dah House specializes in Old Navajo, Zuni, and Hopi jewelry, baskets, and pottery.

Boothill graveyard in Tombstone.

The Third Street Antique Mall features several dealers under one roof, giving you a wide selection of quality pieces. Here, you can purchase anything from a pocket watch to furniture to Native American artifacts. It is located above the Museum of the West at 109 South Third Street.

On the way out of town on Highway 80 is the spot where many of the victims of Tombstone's wild era have come to rest. The Boothill Graveyard has about 250 tombstones, complete with interesting epitaphs. A small guide brochure is available that will make your walk around the graveyard more enjoyable. This guide offers many stories, both humorous and tragic, of those resting in the graveyard, including the story of Billy Kinsman: "He was shot by a woman much older than he, who was jealously in love with him." Also resting in the graveyard are Dutch Annie and the victims of the gunfight at the OK Corral.

In addition to the many places to eat or go shopping in Tombstone, there are a few Bed & Breakfast inns, motels, and campgrounds in the vicinity. For information about Tombstone, contact the Chamber of Commerce at 520-457-9317 or the Visitors Center at 520-457-3929.

Bisbee

Directions: Take I-10 east to Benson, exit 303 and go through town and head south on Highway 80, approximately 95 miles southeast of Tucson.

If you want to take a stroll back to the late nineteenth century, or just escape the heat of a Tucson summer, the town of Bisbee is the perfect year-round getaway. The city is located at 5,300 feet in the Mule Mountains, and was originally home to the Apache Indians. The hour and a half trip from Tucson is well worth the drive, not only for the natural beauty of the mountains, but also for the charming historic architecture that makes Bisbee such a unique community.

Lending the area an Old World charm are the many attractive Victorian homes that line the hillsides outside of Bisbee. Although life in Bisbee has changed drastically since the early part of the century the city's architecture has not. Art galleries abound, miners' boarding houses have been transformed into quaint bed and breakfast inns, and old saloons are now shops and cafes.

Bisbee was originally founded as a mining city in the late 1800s. Phelps Dodge started mining in the area in 1881, when it formed its wholly owned subsidiary, The Copper Queen Consolidated Mining Company. The company is responsible for the construction of many of the beautiful buildings you'll see throughout Bisbee's downtown, including the Bisbee Mining and Historical Museum and The Copper Queen Hotel.

Although the original downtown area of Bisbee was burned to the ground in 1908, the booming town was nearly restored to its original state by 1910. Copper continued to be extracted from the area until as late as 1975, when it became unprofitable for the company to continue mining. New technologies have given Phelps Dodge reason enough to continue to operate, however, and the company employs about 100 people in Bisbee.

To learn more about mining in Bisbee, there are a few places that are essential to visit. An obvious choice is the Queen Mine Tour. This tour will take you into the now inactive copper mine. You will be outfitted with a raincoat and a hard hat, complete with a headlamp. To make the ride fully comfortable, however, you should wear warm clothing, as the temperature underground remains at a cool 47°F. A veteran miner will be your guide, and will provide you with historical facts and information on the mining process on your way down into the mine. As you ride on an original "man car," you can peer to the side and see displays of blasting and drilling techniques and a reconstructed elevator with level station. Together, these exhibits give you a close and comprehensive look at underground mining of the past. You may need to call ahead for reservations, especially during holidays, at 520-432-2071.

Another informational adventure in mining operations is the Lavender Pit Open Mine Bus Tour (520-432-2071). You will be amazed at how a landscape that once looked so invincible has been manipulated and transformed into a huge, man-made canyon. From this impressive pit, countless tons of low grade ore has been economically extracted. Although the pit has a purple hue, it is actually named for Phelps Dodge executive, Harrison Lavender. This interesting tour leaves daily at noon from the Queen Mine Building.

To experience the whole story of Bisbee in about an hour, visit the Bisbee Mining and Historical Museum. The Museum displays are extremely creative and well-executed. Clothing of the early settlers, minerals from the area, and hundreds of old photographs help to tell the story of Bisbee.

Because Bisbee was quite culturally diverse at the beginning of this century, the museum has set up an interesting display that describes the discrimination suffered by the many immigrants that came to Bisbee hoping for a better life. Other interesting displays include Community Life, Children of Bisbee, and The 1917 Strike. The latter exhibit illustrates the strike which resulted in the deportation of a thousand striking miners in an effort to "save the city from a communist threat."

The Mulheim Heritage House Museum is another attraction in Bisbee that can help put you in touch with the town's early years. The ten-room home was donated to the City of Bisbee in 1975 by the Mulheim family and is a Registered National Historic Site. The Bisbee Council on the Arts & Humanities worked diligently to restore the home to its original Queen Anne-style elegance, then opened it as a museum in 1980. When you enter the museum, you will appreciate how successful the Council's efforts have been.

The Mulheims' story is one of success as well. Joseph

M. Mulheim Sr. emigrated to Bisbee from Switzerland in 1883, and immediately began brewing beer. For four years, hardworking miners happily drank the beer that Mulheim brewed, then the entrepreneur turned his energies to investing in real estate and mining. The Mulheims laid the foundation of their four-room house in 1898. As the family grew, six more rooms were added, until the home was finally completed in 1915. Guided tours leave daily, and the house may be reserved for special events by contacting the Council on the Arts & Humanities at 520-432-7071.

18 Steps, on Main Street, is a good choice for lunch or dinner (520-432-5155). The menu here includes a little bit of everything and some dishes are quite innovative. Also for dinner, many people recommend Café Roka. In fact, this is

one of the "Top One Hundred Restaurants" in Arizona. Since Café Roka is so popular, be sure to call ahead for reservations at 520-432-5153. Although it is new to the area, The High Desert Inn is sure to become a favorite – the cuisine is excellent, with a decidedly French flair. Call for reservations at 520-432-1442.

Lodging options abound in Bisbee. For a

A view of Bisbee from a nearby hill.

historic and rustic experience, check into The Copper Queen Hotel. The hotel hasn't changed much since the early mining days, and is conveniently located in the center of town. Call 1-800-247-5829 or 520-432-2216 for information.

Another favorite stop is the School House Inn, located a short distance from downtown at 818 Tombstone Canyon Drive. This quaint and relaxing B&B was originally the town's schoolhouse, and was constructed in 1918. The inn's nine rooms – including the History, Reading, and Music rooms – are very spacious, and all have private baths. The breakfast here is extensive, and is as wonderful as the view from the balcony. Call the inn at 520-432-2996 or 1-800-537-4333 for current room rates. For a complete listing of area hotels and B&Bs, check with The Bisbee Chamber of Commerce at 520-432-5421.

Tubac and Tumacacori

Directions: Take I-10 east to I-19 south and get off at exit 34, approximately 40 miles south of Tucson.

Tubac is the oldest city in Arizona, and has been part of the United States since it was acquired in the Gadsen Purchase in 1854. It is likely that Tubac was once the home of the ancient Hohokam tribe from 300 to 1500 A.D. The Ootam (Pima and Tohono O'odham) arrived sometime in the 1300s, and traces of their existence are still visible. Today, Tubac is a popular destination for Arizona residents and visitors. The charming streets are lined with shop after shop – more than 80 in all – which feature unique pieces that range from South American fabrics and pottery to hand-crafted furniture. There are also more than 40 art galleries in town that exhibit primarily local works.

To help you navigate your way through Tubac's shopping district, pick up a free copy of the town's well organized map at the Chamber of Commerce. You can also ask a shopkeeper; most stores have a supply of these helpful maps.

One worthwhile stop to make is at Tortuga Books, set just off Tubac Road. The selection is impressive, as there are many one-of-a-kind books, cards, music, and pieces of fine art. Another good place to visit is the Country Shop, which you'll see in Tubac Plaza. Here, you will find an excellent selection of Mexican crafts, housewares, furniture, and jewelry. Many Gatherings, located near Tortuga Books, has an interesting selection of women's and children's clothing, some of which is created by local artists. If you want a great sampling of Southwestern foods, Chile Pepper on Tubac Road has more than its share of gourmet Southwestern products.

Despite the fabulous shopping for which Tubac is known, the area has quite a bit of history that is sometimes overlooked. To begin to explore the rich history of Tubac, head to The Presidio Museum. Established in 1964, the Presidio Museum is located in the Tubac Presidio State Historic Park, and contains Native American, Spanish Colonial, Mexican Republican, and Anglo Territorial exhibits. If you want to continue your adventure, pick up the Tubac Historical Society's brochure, "A Walking Tour of Historical Tubac." This helpful guide costs only a quarter, and will provide you with a heap of interesting information about the town.

This walking tour will guide you around "Old Town," where you will be amazed by the many historic buildings that now house art galleries and shops. Most of these were erected shortly after Tubac became part of the U.S. One of the most interesting parts of the tour is St. Ann's Catholic Church. It is a light-yellow structure that's full of charm.

Be sure to check out the ruins of the original Spanish fort established in 1751, located in the oldest state park in Arizona – Tubac Presidio State Historic Park. The park has picnic tables that are available for use daily from 8 a.m to 5 p.m. If you'd rather dine in, there is a wonderful restaurant located in the Tubac Golf Resort: La Montura. The rock floors and the converted horse stalls of La Montura, along with its delicious food, combine to create a quite pleasurable dining experience. You will have to drive out of Tubac to reach the golf resort. Turn at the arch at the entrance of the club. For more information, call 520-398-2211.

If you want to continue learning about the history of the area, take the four and a half mile Juan Bautista de Anza National Historic Trail. This is part of the National Historic Trail that led from Nogales to San Francisco. As you proceed, you will see some archaeological ruins along the trail. The trail crosses the San Pedro River several times, but unless it's been raining hard, this should not impede your

Tumacacori Mission near Tubac.

Ed Armstrong

progress. Eventually, the trail leads to the beautiful Tumacacori National Historical Park that lies to the south.

A visit to the Tumacacori Mission is well worth the effort you make to get there. In 1691, Padre Eusebio Kino, visited the site on horseback and envisioned the placement of a church to help serve the smaller mission outposts in the area. The surrounding environment had all the elements required to support a main church: a nearby river, sufficient vegetation to sustain livestock and a small Tohono O'odham village. So, the Mission Los Angeles de Guevavi was established in the area in 1701. This first mission was abandoned in 1772 for reasons that remain unclear, and the Tumacacori Mission was built sometime in the late 1700s. When visiting this mission, be sure to take a look at the adobe walls, which are an incredible six feet thick.

Another place to check out is the Tubac Center for the Arts, where exhibits change several times a year. Shows include the Craft Invitational show and sale, and the annual Arizona Aqueous National Juried Watermedium Show, which includes any work that involves waterbased paints on a paper product. There are also several musical and theatrical performances throughout the year. For more information contact the Center at 520-398-2371.

Whatever you choose to do in Tubac – shop, explore history, or both – you'll soon come to understand the village motto: "Where history and art come together."

Patagonia

Directions: Take I-10 east to exit 281 heading south on Highway 83. Turn right on Highway 82, approximately 60 miles southeast of Tucson.

Situated just 18 miles north of the Mexico border, Patagonia is one of the most beautiful towns around Tucson. It is located in a small valley that's bordered by the Santa Rita Mountains to the north and the Patagonia Mountains to the south. One of the tallest peaks in Arizona, Mt. Wrightson, stands nearby at 9,453 feet, and can be seen from anywhere in town. Because Patagonia itself is at an elevation of 4,044 feet, it is an average of ten degrees cooler than Tucson, and sometimes has snow in the winter.

Patagonia is known worldwide primarily for the abundance of birds that choose to migrate through the valley. Over 250 species are spotted annually, including such rare birds as the Grey Hawk, Green Kingfisher, Thick-billed Kingbird, Northern Beardless Tyrannulet, and even the Violet-crowned Hummingbird. With this abundant diversity, it's no wonder that many of those who visit Patagonia are avid birdwatchers.

An excellent place to birdwatch, or just take a relaxing hike, is the Patagonia Sonoita Creek Preserve that's owned by the Nature Conservancy. This international non-profit conservation organization is devoted to the protection of rare plants and animals, and the Patagonia Sonoita Creek Preserve is one of its nine Arizona preserves. One of the richest habitats in Arizona, the preserve is located on Sonoita Creek. The very best time for birding is March through September. During the monsoon season (usually late July and August), it's a good idea to wear bug repellent on excursions of any sort.

As you walk along the trails in the preserve, you'll notice many huge Fremont cottonwood trees. These impressive trees reach heights of over 100 feet, and some are more than 130 years old. Other plant life includes the Arizona black walnut, canyon hackberry, and several varieties of willow.

Though you may not spot them, mountain lions, bobcats, javelina, coyotes, white-tail deer, and desert tortoises also make their homes in the preserve. Even rattlesnakes have been known to live here. Because the stream that runs through the preserve is perennial, it is one of the few places that can support the four species of endangered fish that inhabit it.

Surrounding Patagonia are two well-loved aquatic attractions, including Lake Patagonia and Parker Canyon Lake, 14 and 40 miles out of town, respectively. Both lakes provide facilities for fishing, boating, camping, and picnicking. During the summer weekends, these lakes can be slightly crowded, so it's a good idea to visit them early in the morning.

Since the town is surrounded by state and federal land, there are many places to hike in the Patagonia area. Whether you want to go backpacking overnight, on an all-day hike, or just take a quick walk, you will find the trail that's perfect for you. Many mountain bikers and horseback riders share the trails as well. If you don't have much time, but want to get out into the mountains, there is a two-hour driving loop that winds through several old mining towns and miles of beautiful terrain.

If you simply want to enjoy the town itself, you have some wonderful options. A Patagonia Affair – The Fall Festival is an annual event held during the third weekend of October (call 520-394-0066 for information). Music, food, vendors, and talented artisans gather on the streets for the weekend from 10 a.m. to 5 p.m. Several galleries are also open to the public throughout the year. The Mesquite Grove Gallery (520-394-2358) is home to many local artists' work and is a great place to buy or browse. While the hours of operation here are somewhat limited during the summer, owner Regina Medley will be happy to open the gallery if you give her a call at 520-394-2732. The Patagonia Gallery (520-394-2732) is also well worth visiting.

Another interesting stop is Graycie's Gift & Candle Shop at 60 Naugle Ave. (520-394-2035). Graycie will be happy to give you a quick tour of her home that she has converted into a gallery/museum/shop. Her sand masks and other works are as original and charming as Graycie herself.

Next door to Graycie's is a wonderful restaurant, The Ovens of Patagonia, located at 292 Naugle Ave. (520-394-2433). They offer a delicious variety of home-baked goods and a full menu for breakfast, and the coffee and service are equally good. The Ovens is also open for lunch, and you shouldn't leave town without trying at least one piece of their extraordinary fruit pies. If you prefer to picnic, pick up some lunch goodies at Red Mountain Foods (520-394-2786), a small yet complete natural foods store at the corner of Highway 82 and 4th Street.

If you're lucky enough to have time to stay overnight in Patagonia, there are several wonderful bed and breakfasts from which to choose. It is important to make reservations well in advance, as places are often booked throughout the season. A favorite and beautiful B&B is the Little House (520-394-2493). It's located in the center of Patagonia and offers a great deal of charm and privacy. Relax into the comfortable sitting area, lounge before the fireplace, or write a letter on the patio. Each room has a private bath. There is also a lovely common courtyard where hummingbirds come to feed. Coffee and tea are delivered to you in the morning, while the owners, Don and Doris Wenig, prepare a delicious breakfast. Room rates are $67.25 for two people and $56 for one.

The Duquesne House Bed & Breakfast (520-394-2732) is also located in town on the original main street of Patagonia. The turn-of-the-century adobe structure was once an apartment building for miners. Today, it is a quaint and homey place that provides a sitting room, bedroom, and private bath with each accommodation. In the winter, the rooms are heated with funky old woodburning stoves. The cost is $65 for up to two people.

If you'd prefer to rent an intimate cabin, Rothrock Cottage and Adobe provide private guest accommodations. The two-bedroom cottage is located on a quiet residential street, just adjacent to the Patagonia Sonoita Creek Preserve. Rothrock Adobe is a larger, territorial-style, L-shaped adobe house, with two spacious bedrooms and a private patio. Both have full baths and complete kitchens stocked with breakfast goodies. The cost is $75 for up to two people and $20 for each additional person. You can reserve the cottage or adobe by calling 520-394-2952.

Sonoita

Directions: Take I-10 east to exit 281 heading south on Highway 83, approximately 40 miles southeast of Tucson.

On your way to or from Patagonia, you must plan to stop in the nearby town of Sonoita – a great place to go to enjoy wine tastings and great food. While most people don't associate southern Arizona with wine, the region's temperate climate is ideal for growing grapes.

The community of Elgin, just outside of Sonoita, is home to three excellent wineries: Sonoita Vineyards, Santa Cruz Winery, and Callaghan Vineyards. In addition to the fine wines available here, you'll also find Karen's Wine Country Café. A highly acclaimed and truly excellent restaurant, Karen's offers food that is fresh, delicious, and very original. Because tables here are in strong demand, it's a good idea to make reservations in advance by calling 520-455-5282.

Another Sonoita favorite, Er Pastaro, is open for dinner only. New York chef Giovanni Shifano and his wife, Karin, create fresh, flavorful Roman-style pasta and other innovative Italian dishes, including many vegetarian options. Many celebrities, Giovanni's fans

Wine tasting in the Sonoita wine country.

from the big city, visit when they're in the area. Their autographed photos hang on the walls over the red and white checked tablecloths in this distinctly Italian atmosphere. Again, we recommend making reservations at Er Pastaro before heading out to Sonoita. Call them at 520-455-5821.

Plan to set aside an entire afternoon when heading out to Sonoita on a wine tasting expedition, not only because the town is an hour away, but also because you'll probably want to complete your experience by sampling some of the outstanding cuisine at Karen's or Er Pastaro.

Amerind Foundation and Museum

Directions: 64 miles east of Tucson on I-10. Take exit 318 (to Dragoon) and go east 1 mile to Amerind Foundation turnoff, making a left at the sign.

Phone: 520-586-3666

Hours: (Sept.-May) Open daily 10 a.m. to 4 p.m. (June-August) W-Sun 10 a.m. to 4 p.m. Closed on major holidays.

Admission: Adults $3, senior citizens and children 12-18 $2, per person group rate $2, children under 12 free.

Much of the Southwest's appeal stems from the Native American cultures that have existed in this region for many centuries. Founded in 1937 by William S. Fulton, the Amerind (American Indian) Foundation is devoted to the study of Native American culture and history, and operates a fine museum and art gallery depicting past and present ways of Native American life.

Housed in a Spanish colonial Revival-style building, the museum exhibits archaeological collections, photographs, and time-line displays that offer a sense of connection to the history and culture of America's first natives. Some examples include the fine beadwork of the Plains Indians, weavings by Navajo craftspeople, and snowshoe-making tools of the Cree.

Also located in the Foundation building is the Amerind Art Gallery, which features Western and Southwestern art by artists such as Frederick Remington and William Leigh. The Museum Store carries crafts from the greater Southwest, and has a fine selection of books on history and Native American culture.

We recommend taking a picnic lunch along when you head out to the Amerind Foundation. There are lovely picnic facilities on the grounds, and you won't find much food along the way.

One popular detour – either on your way to, or return from, the Amerind Foundation – is to the one-of-a-kind Singing Wind Bookshop (520-586-2425), located just outside of Benson, Arizona. Specializing in Western Americana, this bookstore is run by the animated and impassioned Winifred Bundy, who operates both the store and the 640-acre working cattle ranch upon which it is located. Winifred's eclectic inventory is comprised of an excellent collection of Western literature, and many books on the

Amerind Foundation Museum complex in Dragoon.

wildlife, history, and geology of Arizona, and her international clientele has included visitors from Russia, Switzerland, France, Germany, Italy, and Japan.

To reach the ranch, take Interstate 10 to the Ocotillo Road exit, Exit 34, then head 2.3 miles north away from town. Turn right at the sign that reads "Singing Wind Bookshop," and continue 1/2 mile until you reach the gate. Open the gate, and be sure to close it behind you, as wayward cows are always eager to escape. Because Winifred's time is split between the bookstore and the ranch, we strongly recommend that you call before heading out to Singing Wind, both to confirm directions and to be sure that Winifred will be available to meet you.

Directions: Drive east on I-10, 81 miles to Willcox, exit 340. Go south from Willcox on 186/181, then east to the Monument.

Phone: 520-824-3560

For awe-inspiring rock formations and 111 miles of beautiful trails, Chiricahua National Monument in the Chiricahua Wilderness is the perfect getaway. Dubbed "The Land of the Standing-Up Rocks" by the Apache, the Chiricahuas are a unique sight to behold and explore, and are located only two hours outside of Tucson.

The immense spires of volcanic rock have been curiously worn by erosion to resemble stacks of pancakes – some as tall as 9,000 feet. Equally mysterious, the forest in which the Chiricahuas rise is affected by such odd weather patterns that spring and fall occur simultaneously. In the spring, it is not unusual to see new foliage growing alongside yellowing and reddish leaves. During the monsoon season, from July through September, dramatic afternoon storms further enhance the beauty of the natural terrain.

Rock formations at the Chiricahua National Monument.

In addition to the beautiful landscape and vegetation of the Chiricahua Wilderness, several interesting animal species can be spotted in the area. Deer, peccaries, and lizards roam about, and you may even get to observe the athletic prowess of coatimundies up in the trees. Mexico's version of a raccoon, coatimundies have long, banded tails and pointed snouts, and often travel in packs of four to 25. The Chiricahuas also attract a wide variety of bird species as detailed in the section on birdwatching in the *Outdoor Activities* section of this book.

For a close-up look at the wonders of this wilderness area, head out onto the Chiricahua Crest

Walter H. Saenger

Trail. From the north end of the monument, you can reach the trail from Rustler Park. For a scenic drive, travel along Pinery Canyon Road, or if you would prefer to walk, pick up the trail at Morse Canyon Trailhead at the end of West Turkey Creek Road. This trail climbs up to a gorgeous saddle near Johnson Peak and then heads east to Monte Vista Peak. It is a four-mile, relatively steep hike full of rewarding views.

The hike from Massai Point – starting at 6,870 feet and descending through the Heart of Rocks, then down along the creek to the Visitors Center – is also a favorite. The Echo Canyon Trail provides yet another good day hike. This hike evokes a mild sense of adventure as you make your way among fantastic rock formations and squeeze through narrow passageways. The loop is 3.5 miles long and returns on the Hailstone Trail, a fairly steep grade that goes through Rhyolite Canyon. The trail starts right out of the Echo Canyon parking area and can be a hot one in the summer. Whenever you visit, take lots of water and beware of the sun.

If you have a more substantial hike in mind, or even some overnight backpacking, be sure to stop by the Visitors Center and pick up their thorough guide. The guide is a bargain at just 25¢, and can save you the worry of losing your way. It will also show you where to find the best places to picnic or camp.

Willcox

On your way to or from the Chiricahua National Monument, be sure to make a stop at the junction of Willcox. The area surrounding this small town was considered by all Apaches to be a sacred and holy place. In fact, Geronimo once wrote that he wished to spend his last days there and, to be buried among the mountains. Given this reverence, it's not surprising that there were many battles between the U.S. Cavalry and the Chiricahua Apaches when settlers began moving into the region. Commemorative sites throughout the area acknowledge and memorialize these battles.

Originally a small construction camp for the Southern Pacific Railroad in 1880, Willcox was eventually settled by cattle ranchers who sucessfully established nearby ranches. Today, the small town of Willcox still has some of the largest cattle ranches in the state of Arizona, and continues to ship cattle to other parts of the country via the railroad.

In addition to having a reputation for raising fine cattle, Willcox is also known around the state for its delicious apples. Once thought to be an improbable industry because of the Arizona sun, the apple growing business is thriving in the Willcox area. For a fresh jug of cider or a plump apple pie, stop by the Stout Cider Mill (520-384-3696) located at exit 340 off of I-10.

Born in Willcox, Rex Allen was a famous cowboy singer during the '40s and '50s, singing such songs as the "Streets of Laredo," which he made famous. Allen also did a little acting, starring in the television series *Frontier Doctor* in the mid-1950s, and many may recognize his voice as the narrator Walt Disney's nature films. The Rex Allen Museum (520-384-4583) is located at 150 N. Railroad Avenue, and has such memorabilia from Allen's past as saddles, guitars, movie posters and photos, and even a buggy that was used in *Frontier Doctor*. The museum is open from 10 a.m. to 4 p.m. daily, and admission is $3 per person, or $5 per family.

Near the Rex Allen Museum are many older buildings, one of which is the Willcox Commercial Store, where Geronimo is reputed to have shopped. Built in 1881, this dry goods store is still in operation, and is considered to be the oldest commercial building in use in Arizona.

Ghost towns are – in many cases – all that is left to remind us of once-successful towns that flourished with community and business. Arizona has many of these towns within its borders, primarily due to the large number of mining operations that began production, then quickly folded when the ore ran out. Listed below are three ghost towns that are located relatively close to one another along the gravel road known as "the ghost town trail," just outside of Tombstone.

For more information on Arizona ghost towns, you can write or call the Arizona Office of Tourism at 1100 West Washington, Phoenix, AZ 85001, 602-542-8687, or pick up a book on ghost towns, such as Philip Varney's *Arizona Ghost Towns and Mining Camps.*

Gleeson

Located 16 miles east of Tombstone on "the ghost town trail," Gleeson is named after prospector John Gleeson, who mined the area for turquoise in 1900. The town eventually fell into its current run-down state after a large copper mining operation closed in approximately 1957.

What remains of Gleeson are several adobe walls, a burned-out jail, the old saloon, and two cement columns that once supported an archway that formed the entrance to the school house. The largest adobe structure here was once the town hospital for the early settlers. There is also a hillside cemetery, complete with weathered grave markers and tattered fences.

If you are in the Gleeson area or visiting Tombstone, you may want to take a side trip to the small and very interesting rattlesnake shop owned by John and Sandy Weber. With everything from hand-made necklaces and earrings to sporty bows and ties made from the slithering reptile, John & Sandy's Rattlesnake & Apache Indian Crafts Shop will surprise you with its selection of rattlesnake curios. The shop is open from dawn to dusk for business and browsing, and visitors are always welcome.

Courtland

Languishing between the ghost towns of Pearce and Gleeson, Courtland was named after Courtland Young, a mining engineer and part owner of the Great Western Mining Company around 1909. Courtland, which once had a population of 2,000, eventually fell into ghost town status in about 1942. Set back next to the Dragoon Mountains, the ghost town has a few decrepit store buildings, and a jailhouse that is still partially standing.

Pearce

Located at the end of "the ghost town trail," Pearce was established when a rancher by the name of John Pearce discovered gold in the area in 1894. While a few people still live in this town, the Pearce Old Store, which was the main tourist attraction of Pearce, closed a few years back.

While the old adobe buildings have worn with time, the town's post office and store still stand. Further along, you can still see the remains of what was once the Commonwealth Mine and Mill. Visiting the ancient, but still used cemetery, you will discover the tombstones of Abraham Lincoln's bodyguard, and a few Union and Confederate soldiers.

Ghost Towns

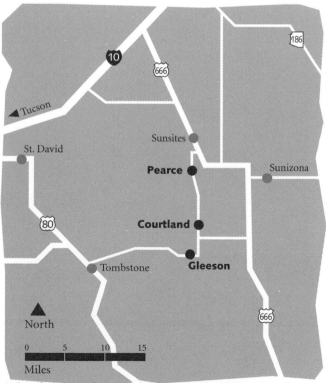

At time of printing, Highway 666 is being renumbered to Highway 191.

Coronado National Memorial

Directions: Head east on I-10 until you get to Highway 90 (approximately 65 miles), head south to Sierra Vista. The Coronado National Memorial turnoff is approximately 12 miles south of Sierra Vista on Highway 92. The Visitors Center is another 4.5 miles.

Located in the Huachuca Mountains, Coronado National Memorial is named after the Spanish explorer, Francisco Vásquez de Coronado, who journeyed through this area in 1540 looking for the legendary seven cities of gold. The nearly 5,000-acre memorial is maintained by the National Park Service, and has a Visitors Center (520-366-5515) that features exhibits on local plant and animal life, and on the history of the region.

One of the highlights of this area is the view from the top of the 6,846-foot Coronado Peak. From there, you can observe the horizon as it extends beyond Arizona and into Mexico. To get to Coronado Peak from the Visitors Center, you can either drive your car the 3.2 miles on a dirt road to Montezuma Pass, or make the moderate 3.1 mile (1,300-foot ascent) hike via Joe's Canyon Trail. From the Pass, the Peak lies a half-mile away, along the Coronado Peak Trail (280-foot ascent). Along the path are shaded rest areas and signs describing some of the Huachuca Mountains' natural features, and tidbits about the Coronado Expedition.

For information regarding the many trails in the Huachuca Mountains, you may want to purchase Leonard Taylor's *Hiker's Guide to the Huachuca Mountains* at one of the local bookstores.

The Arizona environment isn't made up of deserts and mountains alone. The valleys southeast of Tucson also have natural grassland areas.

Fort Huachuca

Directions: Head east on I-10 until you get to Highway 90, then head south to Sierra Vista and turn right on Fry Blvd.; this will take you to the main gate.

Phone: 520-533-5736

Hours: M-F 9 a.m. to 4 p.m., Saturday 1 to 4 p.m.

Admission: Free

Originally intended as a temporary camp for the U.S. Cavalry, Fort Huachuca was established in 1877 to prevent

northern Indians tribe from crossing the border into Mexico and raiding settlements there, and to protect new American settlements from attack. It was from Fort Huachuca that the campaign against Geronimo was led, until he surrendered in September 1886.

Fort Huachuca was also home to the "Buffalo Soldiers," a group of African-American soldiers who formed the 10th Cavalry Division. It was in 1916 that they assisted General Pershing as he pursued Pancho Villa into Mexico.

While the fort did close after WWII, it reopened again in 1953 to serve the Army as a testing site for new electronic devices. With 73,000 acres, the fort is still used today to train troops, and specializes in communication and intelligence. In fact, many of the troops from Desert Shield and Desert Storm came from Fort Huachuca.

To get a better sense of the fort's history, you should visit the Fort Huachuca Historical Museum. The many photos, exhibits, and artifacts provide a good overview of the life and times at the fort, from its early days to the present. The museum is located in two buildings at the corner of Boyd and Grierson Streets, about 2.5 miles in from the main gate at Sierra Vista.

Mt. Lemmon

Directions: Take Tanque Verde East to Catalina Highway.
Turn left on Catalina Highway, and drive 30 miles to the top of
Mt. Lemmon.

Mt. Lemmon is a cool oasis in the summer and a nearby place to find snow in the winter. Located in the Santa Catalinas, the mountain is named after Sara Lemmon, the first woman to climb the peak. She and her husband spent their 1881 honeymoon trying to climb to the summit – twice – and finally succeeded by riding over the north side on horseback.

Mt. Lemmon is the southernmost ski area in the continental United States, and is the only U.S. peak named for the first woman who climbed it.

Today, the 30-mile road up Mt. Lemmon will take you from the desert valley through five distinct vegetative zones – all of which you would experience on the much longer drive from Tucson to the Canadian border. As you drive (or bicycle, if you feel like a good climb) over the south side of the mountain, you will first encounter the area's signature saguaros and century plants, then silverleaf oaks, and finally ponderosa pines, Douglas firs, and quaking aspens. There are also several viewpoints on the way up that offer spectacular perspectives on the valley below. Windy Point is particularly breathtaking. It takes only an hour to see all of this, so it's no wonder that Mt. Lemmon has become one of the most popular escapes for visitors and Tucsonans alike.

As you can imagine, the mountain offers great places to climb, hike, ski, and mountain bike, all of which are discussed in the *Outdoor Activities* section of this book. If you just want to take a journey to cooler weather for a leisurely day or to go skiing at Mt. Lemmon Ski Valley when the conditions permit, Mt. Lemmon is a perfect destination.

Like a lot of ski areas, Mt. Lemmon Ski Valley runs its lifts during the summers, the other option for those that don't want to hike the steep trails which lead to the top. In addition to being less strenuous, the lift also offers fabulous views – the whole way up. It's a one-mile ride to the top, and it takes approximately 25 minutes to reach the 9,100-foot peak.

There is also fishing to be done on Mt. Lemmon. On your way up, about when you reach fir trees, you will see signs pointing the way to Rose Canyon Lake. This mountain lake is stocked with trout and is a popular spot for fishing. If you are really serious about making a catch, you'll be wise to arrive early in the morning, as people go to the lake to picnic, play with the dog, or just hang out. A nearby campground is a great place to spend the night; there's a small fee for camping.

You'll find other campgrounds on your way up the mountain where you can stay free of charge. The first one is located at Molino Basin, just a few miles from the base. There is no drinking water available here, so be sure to bring plenty of your own. The next campground is the General Hitchcock Campground at an elevation of 6,000 feet, and drinking water is often available at this site.

Close to the top of Mt. Lemmon is the tiny town of Summerhaven, which has a lodge, small cabins, campgrounds, a gas station, and restaurants. For delicious baked goods and a cup of coffee, there is a newer little place, Kimball Springs Café and Bakery. It is the second restaurant on the left as you proceed through Summerhaven. They also serve fresh sandwiches and soups, but be sure to sample the orange scones. At Mt. Lemmon Cafe, which is the first place on the left, you can eat some of the best homemade pies that you will ever taste. The cafe also has a lovely porch on which you can bask in the mountain air and sunshine.

Another popular place to enjoy lunch year-round is the Iron Door Restaurant, located at the base of Mt. Lemmon Ski Valley. It, too, has a pleasant and spacious deck where you can enjoy your meal. They serve sandwiches, soups, salads, good cornbread and chili, and beer. Be sure to note, however, that neither the Ski Valley nor the Iron Door Restaurant accepts credit cards.

Rappel Rock on Mt. Lemmon.

Mike Liebert

Nogales – Sonora, Mexico

Directions: Take I-10 east to I-19 south and take exit 4 off the freeway, approximately 60 miles south of Tucson.

If you're interested in doing some shopping and experiencing a bit of Mexican culture, a visit to the border city of Nogales in Sonora, Mexico is definitely in order. Located just 65 miles south of Tucson via I-19, Nogales is an easy and rewarding day trip destination for the whole family. To keep things simple, we recommend leaving your car in one of the pay parking lots on the U.S. side of the border. You can park for the entire day for under $5, walk across the border and enjoy the day without worrying about your car. If you do choose to drive into Nogales, however, be sure to purchase Mexican insurance for your vehicle (see the Puerto Peñasco day trip for more information on insurance). There's no need to take your passport along unless you're heading further into Mexico.

Once across the border, your first stop should be Ave. Obregón. On this main artery of Nogales, you'll find countless and varied *tiendas* (stores) and curio shops. These stores are all within close proximity of one another – making shopping both convenient and safe – and they carry a wide variety of items that have been hand-crafted in towns throughout Mexico. When shopping, it's important to keep in mind that you may only bring $400 worth of goods back across the border, per person, per trip.

Hand blown glass, native pottery, wrought iron items, wool rugs, and *Nacimientos* (nativity scenes) are common wares in Nogales, and prices vary between stores. Curio shops sell typical Mexican wares such as leather goods, patterned blankets, ceramics, and folk art. Brand-name liquors are heavily discounted throughout Mexico, but customs officials are strict about the quantity purchased: one liter per person, and then only if you're over 21 years of age. Pure vanilla extract is another inexpensive find. A reminder: bargaining is standard practice in the curio shops, but the better stores are "fixed price" in U.S. dollars. Do try your luck with the vendors, but be aware that true "bargains" are rare.

While it may at first seem that all of the shops in Nogales are alike, there are four must-see merchants that stand out from the rest. Each of these stores carry distinctive Mexican crafts, and cater expressly to their American clientele by speaking fluent English and fixing their prices in dollars.

For collectible art, visit the Lazy Frog at Campillo Street #57. With a wide selection of original art by well-known Mexican artisans, and reproductions of famous folk art, this tienda specializes in unique decorative accessories such as Oaxacan wood carvings and Talavera pottery. Look high and low in this store – you'll find distinctive pieces throughout – and be sure to ask about the background and cultural significance of any items you choose. One example of art with a story at the Lazy Frog is found in the terra cotta artwork of the Ocumicho Indians. Without exception, they include a devil or two in each piece of their artwork, with the hope that the presence of the devil image will keep the real Devil away! Store hours are Monday-Saturday from 10 a.m. to 5 p.m., with a lunch break from 1 to 2 p.m., and closed Sunday.

Young girl selling her wares in Nogales, Sonora, Mexico.

Ed Armstrong

El Sarape, at Ave. Obregón #161, has been in operation since 1942. This family-owned business is the oldest in Nogales, and has carved its niche by specializing in extraordinary pewter picture frames and serving pieces. El Sarape also carries Nogales's finest selection of sterling silver jewelry from Taxco, including the original work of several of the country's well-known designers. Finally, if you're looking for lovely hand-made Mexican garments, this is a great place to find them. Store hours are from 10 a.m. to 6 p.m. daily.

Each room of El Changarro has been painstakingly decorated with one-of-a-kind furnishings and accessories from Central and Southern Mexico. Located at Calle Elias #93, this store is filled with furniture and artwork – in wood, wool, and glass – that has been hand-carved, exquisitely woven, or blown by hand. Once you've chosen your treasures from this trove, El Changarro will handle the logistics of helping you get them across the border in one piece. Store hours are from 10 a.m. to 6 p.m. daily.

You can visit Rusticos de Mexico at two locations in Nogales (Ave. Obregón #167-6, or Pasaje Morelo #73-1), or visit their Tucson location (4664 E. Speedway Blvd., 520-327-4053) to enjoy the Mexican shopping experience without crossing the border. Specializing in custom-made furnishings designed by the shop's owner, Rusticos de Mexico also carries many pieces that are hand-crafted in Nogales. Also featured in the store are exact reproductions of works by Diego Rivera and Frida Kahlo on both canvas and furniture. Hand-painted or cloth equipale furniture is also available. Rusticos is open daily, but definitely maintains "Mexican hours." You'll usually find the doors open between 11 a.m. and 5 p.m.

When you're tuckered out from a great day of shopping, you'll want to enjoy some authentic refreshment, and there are several good restaurants from which to choose. Las Brasas, at Maclovio Herrera V Jesus Sigueiros #101, offers tremendous carne asada. Traveling musicians visit this restaurant, but be prepared to pay around $5 per song requested or accepted. Las Brasas is located about 1-1/2 miles from the border, so you'll probably want to take a taxi there.

Two other restaurants favored and frequented by American visitors are Elvira's, on the border at the north end of Ave. Obregón just west of the customs office, and La Roca, located on Calle Elias. Elvira's is famous for its Fish Elvira, and has a dance bar – Kookaracha's – where you can get a taste of the nightlife in Nogales. La Roca is adjacent to El Changarro, and offers fine dining from 11 a.m. to 11 p.m. daily. This unique restaurant is built into the mountainside, and, on Thursday through Saturday evenings, hosts a live band that plays romantic Mexican music. Both of these are within easy walking distance of the border.

A final note: when it comes to your pharmaceutical needs, there's no more affordable place to meet them than in Mexico. So, while you may know that many prescription medicines are available over the counter in Nogales – and at lower prices – you may not necessarily be able to transcend the language barrier to get what you really need. If you plan to pick up some medicine on your trip, try to have your prescription with you when you cross the border, then head to one of these two reputable and English-friendly pharmacies: La Campana, Ave. Obregón & Diaz #13; and Farmacia Galeno, Ave. Obregón #185.

Puerto Peñasco/Rocky Point – Sonora, Mexico

When Tucsonans long for beaches and ocean breezes, their closest option for a seaside retreat is in Mexico, and road trips south of the border are a part of the Tucson lifestyle.

Only four hours southwest of Tucson, 66 miles into Mexico, lies Puerto Peñasco – also known as "Rocky Point" – a fishing village and tourist mecca located on the northern tip of the Sea of Cortez. Much of Puerto Peñasco's authentic Mexican charm remains despite the recent boom in development and influx of Americans. Because this destination is located farther from Tucson than the other day

Organ Pipe cactus.

Ed Armstrong

trips included in this section, your visit to Puerto Peñasco will be more enjoyable when done in two days or more.

You'll reach this small town easily by car from Tucson. Just travel west along Highway 86 through Quijota and Why, then south onto Highway 85, and through beautiful Organ Pipe National Monument to the border town of Sonoyta (not to be confused with Sonoita, near Patagonia). Once you cross the border, continue south on Highway 8 to Puerto Peñasco.

Because Puerto Peñasco is in the *zona libre* or "free zone," you won't need to register your vehicle at the border, and visas are not required for American visitors. You are strongly encouraged, however, to purchase an auto insurance policy that will provide coverage for your vehicle in Mexico either in Tucson, in the town of Why on Highway

86, or on the U.S. side of the border.

The cost for this insurance is minimal; you can get full coverage for 3 days for about $20, and liability for just $12 for most vehicles. If you plan to stay for a week, full coverage insurance is approximately $40, and liability only is about $24. For more information, or to purchase a policy, call Sanborn's Insurance Company at 520-327-1255. Sanborn's is located at 2900 E. Broadway Blvd., Suite 108.

You can also buy insurance at any one of the small agencies you'll see just before you reach the border. Make sure you have proof of ownership and the vehicle ID number before you go to purchase the insurance. If you're renting a car, make sure the rental company allows travel into Mexico, and ask if there are any additional insurance requirements you need to meet.

On the road between Tucson and Puerto Peñasco lie two "must-see" locations: Organ Pipe National Monument, just south of Ajo, Arizona, and "El Pinacate," 30 miles north of your destination. To fully appreciate these extraordinary natural areas, plan to spend about two hours at each site.

At Organ Pipe National Monument, you'll find more than 31 types of cacti and 225 different species of birds, many of which are unique to this area. To fully experience the beauty of this area, head to the Visitors Center just off Highway 85. The center is open from 8 a.m. to 5 p.m., and park rangers are on hand to answer questions and provide information on the monument. There are plenty of camping sites with drinking water available for about $8 per night, and the area is laced with moderately easy hiking trails.

El Pinacate is a dramatic volcanic area with a history that dates back 3,000 years. It's part of 2 million acres that have been designated as the *Biosphera,* or "Biospheric Reserve," that also includes the Gulf of California and the Baja Peninsula. Those with 4-wheel drive vehicles – and a detailed map! – can easily access the area's impressive volcanic craters, lava flows, and more remote points of the Sonoran Desert. Guided tours of the area are also available by contacting Ajo Stage Line (800-942-1981).

Puerto Peñasco's unique location at the top of the sea makes the water relatively calm – perfect for swimming. You will want to take extra precautions if you're in the water when the winds are strong, as the currents can be powerful and dangerous. The water is also ideal for sea kayaking and windsurfing, and other water activities. The extreme tide in Puerto Peñasco make tidal pool exploring one of the more popular beach activities.

Most of the beaches are beautifully pristine, but at certain times of the year, especially during college spring break weeks, they can be crowded and

A whale skeleton at the entrance of CEDO.

noisy. Whenever you visit, it's best to check out many of the beaches to find the one best suited to your tastes before settling in for the day, especially if you're camping.

One very interesting place to visit is CEDO, the Intercultural Center for the Study of Deserts and Oceans. This non-profit organization has played an important role in the conservation of endemic and endangered animals of the area. Their center is located five miles east of town on Playa las Conchas. A 55-foot whale skeleton marks the entrance to the facility. Also on the site is the Earthship CEDO, a solar building constructed of old tires, sand, and aluminum cans as a model of alternative housing. Tours are available, and, though there's no fee for admission, donations are appreciated.

There are many lodging possibilities in Puerto Peñasco, ranging from camping on Sandy Beach to oceanfront condo rentals. Some of the area's best lodging offerings include Costa Brava (011-52-638-3-41-00), within walking distance to curio shops and shrimp vendors in Old Town, the beachfront Playa Bonita (800-569-1797), and the premier hotel, Hotel Plaza Las Glorias (800-544-4686), which overlooks the beach and has a lovely swimming pool. Each of these hotels has a good restaurant and a convenient and safe, central location. For furnished beachfront rentals by the week or weekend, Clifton Management Company (520-886-5716) offers a wide selection of well-maintained properties in the area.

The dining opportunities in Puerto Peñasco are diverse. You can buy fish tacos at a shack on the harbor, or dine in a fine restaurant on Mexican or American cuisine. There are also supermarkets in town if you need provisions for beach camping. Some of our favorite restaurants include La Casa de Capitán (011-52-638-3-56-98) – at Ave. de Agua #1 – which offers spectacular sunset views. El Delfin Amigable (Friendly Dolphin) – at Ave. Alcantar #44 – has a new rooftop dining area and table-side serenades. At The Happy Frog – at Calle Chiapas and Matamoros – chef Rene Munro does wonders with "the local catch," and you'll want to visit Flavio's for lunch – in the Old Town Fish Market – where live music from local bands creates a fun atmosphere.

In addition to the numerous curio shops, Puerto Peñasco has several shops that market wonderfully diverse wares. The Cowboy Shop, or El Rodeo – in the Jim Bur Shopping Center – has a great selection of authentic Huichol Indian Beadwork. Victoria's Hormiga – next to the Friendly Dolphin at Alcontar #53 – carries interesting hand-painted furniture and innovative gifts. Look for the ants painted onto the outside of the building. At Fina Hoyas Studio – near the old port, just past the oil tanks – you'll find original stained glass and metal work by this renowned artist. And Casa Bonita – at the corner of Benito Juarez and 20 de Noviembre – offers a varied collection of reasonably priced, hand-crafted furniture from Southern Mexico.

Outdoor Activities

With an average of 300 days of sunshine per year, Tucson is a magnet destination for those who love the outdoors. With numerous championship golf courses that are rated among the best in the world, hundreds of miles of incomparable hiking, and an abundance of unique wildlife for birdwatchers and naturalists, the region has outdoor activities for everyone. You can also enjoy exceptional cycling on scenic roads and desert trails, horseback riding on mountain ridges, and challenging skiing opportunities. The city's parks also provide great venues for running, skating, or simply hanging around and enjoying the warmth of the sun.

We can't encourage you enough – whatever you're doing outside in Tucson – to wear sunscreen with a high skin protection factor, and to take along (and drink!) more water than you think you'll need. The desert can be extremely hot and dry, and while the area offers virtually limitless opportunities for fun, the dangers of exposure and dehydration are very real.

Golf

Tucson is widely recognized as one of the richest golf regions in the world, with championship courses that host the annual PGA tour, and many others with natural desert beauty and levels of challenge to suit every ambition. If you haven't yet explored the myriad golf opportunities in Tucson, or if it's been awhile since you've taken up your clubs, here are some compelling reminders as to why you simply must return.

Because of the low humidity, Tucson's often extreme temperatures are more comfortable than you would expect. However, because of this dry heat, it's important to drink plenty of water when you're out and about.

El Rio Municipal Golf Course

Address: 1400 W. Speedway Blvd.

Phone: 520-623-6783

Holes: 18, Yards: 6418, Par: 70

Green Fees: Summer $11.75/18, Winter $13.50/20

Cart Fees: $9/14

A favorite year-round course for both Tucsonans and visitors, El Rio offers fairly flat terrain, with many trees and two small lakes that add to the interest and attractiveness of the course. Smaller greens and tight fairways intensify your challenge, and a practice green and well-lit driving range give you an opportunity to perfect your game. A clubhouse is also available.

Fred Enke Municipal Golf Course

Address: 8251 E. Irvington Rd.

Phone: 520-296-8607

Holes: 18, Yards: 6809, Par: 72

Green Fees: Summer $11.75/18, Winter $13.50/20

Cart Fees: $9/14

The Fred Enke Municipal Golf Course is another of the desert's premier courses. With limited turf, well-calculated bunkers and substantial teeing areas, this course offers both large greens and substantial sand traps. You can choose from four teeing areas, and should beware the 4,555-

yard par-4 Number 9. The serious bunkers on this hole make it one the course's more complex offerings. The course also has a nice practice green and a well-lit driving range. For après golf refreshment, head to the on-site bar and grill.

Loews Ventana Canyon Resort

Address: 7000 N. Resort Dr.

Phone: 520-299-2020

Canyon Course

Holes: 18, Yards: 6818, Par: 72

Cart and Green Fees: Summer $45/65, Winter $90/125

One of two beautiful and challenging golf courses designed by Tom Fazio for Loews Ventana, the Canyon Course is offers incredible golfing amid some of the desert's finest scenery. Set in Esperero Canyon, with the Santa Catalina Mountains in the distance, this course – with its dramatic finish on the par-5 Number 18 island green – is sure to leave you yearning to return.

Mountain Course

Holes: 18, Yards: 6926, Par: 72

Cart and Green Fees: Summer $45/65, Winter $90/125

The second – and much more difficult – Tom Fazio course is the Mountain Course. Here, you can try your hand at the widely renowned 100-yard, par-3 signature hole. Fazio's design incorporates the desert's natural landscape to provide additional obstacles that make this one of the area's most formidable courses.

Randolph Municipal Golf Courses

Address: 600 S. Alvernon Way.

Phone: 520-325-2811

North Course

Holes: 18, Yards: 6902, Par: 72

Green Fees: Summer $12.75/20, Winter $14.50/22

Cart Fees: $9/14

The North Course is the longest of Tucson's Municipal courses, and is host to the PING Welch's LPGA Open, and numerous other distinguished championship tournaments.

With carefully maintained greens, trees, and mountain views, this course is a favorite of locals, and also has a lighted driving range, practice green, and a comfortable club house.

South Course

Holes: 18, Yards: 6229, Par: 70
Green Fees: Summer $12.75/20, Winter $14.50/22
Cart Fees: $9/14

If you're new to the game, or just want a quick round of golf, the straightforward layout and smooth terrain of the South Course make it the ideal choice for you. The course shares the facilities available at the North Course, and gives you a similar spectacular perspective on the surrounding mountains.

Santa Rita Country Club

Address: 16461 S. Houghton Rd.
Phone: 520-762-5620
Holes: 18, Yards: 6396, Par: 71
Green Fees: Summer $9/12, Winter $10/16
Cart Fees: $10/16

Set at the foot of the Santa Rita Mountains, the Santa Rita Country Club has some of Arizona's most outstanding bentgrass greens. Because it's nearly 1,000 feet above Tucson, this course is cooler than those on the valley floor, making it a great choice during the warmer weather. Amid the Bermuda fairways, you'll find four rigorous par-3 holes. Warm up on the putting green, enjoy the views of the surrounding mountains and the valley below, then finish off your day with a beverage in the Corona Room Lounge, or lunch in the Desert Dove Restaurant.

Sheraton El Conquistador Resort and Country Club

Resort Course

Address: 10000 N. Oracle Rd.
Phone: 520-544-1770
Holes: 9, Yards: 2788, Par: 35
Cart and Green Fees: Summer $15/25, Winter $40/70

Making use of the property's dramatic natural landscaping

and rolling elevations, the Sheraton El Conquistador's nine-hole, par-34 Resort Course surrounds the Sheraton resort complex itself. Slim fairways and small, exacting greens are woven into the cacti-dotted, fluctuating terrain to create a surprisingly strenuous course. The Resort Course makes for a satisfying contest in and of itself, or will give you a considerable warm-up for a later game.

Silverbell Municipal Golf Course

Address: 3600 N. Silverbell Rd.	
Phone: 520-743-7284	
Holes: 18, Yards: 6824, Par: 72	
Green Fees: Summer $11.75/18, Winter $13.50/20	
Cart Fees: $9/14	

Perched on the west bank of the Santa Cruz River, the Silverbell Municipal course has tremendous views of both the Tucson and Catalina Mountains. The course is open to the public throughout the year, and is reputed to have the toughest par 5 hole in the area – the 17th – which requires especially skillful maneuvering on the third shot. A practice green and lighted driving range are also available, and you can grab a quick meal at the bar and grill before or after your game.

Starr Pass Golf Course

Address: 3645 W. Starr Pass Blvd.	
Phone: 520-670-0400	
Holes: 18, Yards: 6910, Par: 71	
Cart and Green Fees: May 16 - October 15, $48. After October 15, call for winter prices.	

The west side of Tucson is home to yet another outstanding course: Starr Pass. Set in the foothills of the Tucson Mountains, this challenging course is home to the Northern Telecom Open, a stop on the PGA Tour. Integrated into the rocky, cactus-covered, desert landscape by designer Robert Cupp, the course has Bermuda grass fairways and bent-grass greens, which are kept up to PGA standards throughout the year. Many of the greens are elevated, and some tricky surprises await – especially on a particular 325-yard, par 4.

Tucson National Golf Resort

Address: 2727 W. Club Dr.

Phone: 520-297-2271

Holes: 27, Yards: 7108, Par: 73

Cart and Green Fees: Summer M-F $45, Sat-Sun $50, call for winter prices.

Designed in 1960 by Robert Bruce Harris, Tucson National has hosted the prestigious PGA Tour for 17 of the last 29 years. With a traditional layout that has been masterfully enhanced by Von Hagge-Devlin, the 450-acre course has expansive fairways of Bermuda and Penncross bent-grass greens. Whether you're a seasoned pro, or have just taken up your clubs, the lakes, trees, and well-placed bunkers you'll find at Tucson National will give you a new appreciation for the game of golf. A driving range, short-game area and putting green are among the practice facilities available at the course, and the professionals at John Jacob's Golf Learning Center have the experience and expertise to help you push the envelope of your game.

Tucson has some of the best golfing in the nation.

Chris Gould

Desert Golf Tours

Address: 5755 E. River Rd., # 1602

Phone: 520-577-9526, 1-800-544-9145, Fax 520-744-8481

Hours: Daily 7 a.m. to 6 p.m.

Desert Golf Tours is a complete golf vacation planner that offers customized tour packages throughout Southern Arizona for any size group. Its services include arranging lodging, transportation, advance tee times, tournaments and other related programs.

Fantasy Golf Tours

Address: P.O. Box 30073

Phone: 520-296-7130, 1-800-477-7130, Fax 520-795-0949

Hours: Daily 7 a.m. to 6 p.m.

Specializing in providing golf packages and handling group tours and tournament/corporate outings, Fantasy Golf tours also coordinates PGA group exhibitions and lessons, on-course video/photos, and shuttle service arrangements. Spouse programs are also available.

Tee Time Arrangers & Tours, Inc.

Address: 6286 E. Grant Rd.

Phone: 520-296-4800, 1-800-742-9939, Fax 520-886-1067

Hours: Summer M-F 8 a.m. to 3 p.m., Winter M-F 8 a.m. to 5 p.m.

This golf information center offers both standard and custom golf packages, and can arrange tournaments, and advance tee times, in addition to providing VIP corporate services. A realty/relocation consultant can also help you find homes located on golf courses.

Directions: From the center of town, head west on Speedway and follow signs to Gates Pass. Go over Gates Pass and go right on Kinney Road. This is the dramatic mountain route. From the south side of town, go west on Ajo Rd. (Hwy. 86) to Kinney Rd. and turn right. Proceed about 5 miles to Visitors Center.

The impressive views you'll see on the drive over Gates Pass make it a popular spot to stop and enjoy the splendor of the desert, especially at sunset. The western branch of Saguaro National Park offers a breathtaking perspective on the Tucson Mountains. Saguaros cover the mountainsides in greater density than they do in the East Park, and sensational peaks line the background. There are great views of Avra Valley from most of the Park, along with several hiking and picnic areas.

Hiking the Hugh Norris Trail is an excellent way to familiarize yourself with the area, because you can see just about everything from the ledge along which it runs. The first part of the hike is strenuous, but flattens out just a bit as you proceed along the ridge. Eventually, the trail leads to the top of Wasson Peak at 4,687 feet, and the view from here is well worth the five-mile climb. You can reach the trailhead by continuing past the Visitors Center on Kinney Road until you reach Bajada Loop Drive. Parking is right next to the trailhead.

The Valley View Overlook Trail that's also off the Bajada Loop Drive is fairly short and offers an excellent look at the giant saguaros that rise up from steep, rocky hillsides. You can also check out the grand geological formations that make up the Tucson Mountains. These peaks, which abruptly rise from the valley floor, were formed from ten to 20 million years ago.

If you're in the mood for an easy stroll, try the Desert Discovery Nature Trail. Located just off of Kinney Road, the entrance to this trail is well marked. If you'd rather drive than hike, the Bajada Loop Drive offers amazing scenery. It is a six-mile,

177

graded, and unpaved road that will give you a thorough immersion in the saguaro habitat. The saguaro has always been a symbol, and an intricate part, of the desert ecosystem. Its fruit is also important to members of the Tohono O'odham Nation, who use it to make wine for their rain ceremonies.

To learn more about the saguaro and other facets of the desert, be sure to stop off at the new Red Hills Visitors Center. It too, is located right off of Kinney Road and is clearly marked. The main exhibit is a re-creation of a segment of the Sonoran Desert – complete with indigenous flora and fauna. Four color monitors surround the exhibit and display two-minute informational videos on the Saguaro National Park. As you proceed through the exhibit, you can see a realistic rendition of life underground in the desert. A cross-section of the desert segment reveals burrowing animals – such as rattlesnakes and bugs – and you can also view the inside of a saguaro. The exhibit provides you with a great opportunity to see desert life up close.

Also in the Red Hills Visitors Center, you can pick up all the necessary maps to make your way around the park. If you would like to know more about the landscape, you can purchase an excellent little guide, the *Bajada Loop Drive*, for only $1. There is also a nice selection of nature guides, and even children's desert books, in the gift shop.

The Sonoran Desert is the only place in the world where the giant saguaro cacti grow. The two locations that comprise the Saguaro National Park, located east and west of Tucson, have the largest concentration of these cacti.

Saguaro National Park East

Directions: Travel east on Broadway to Old Spanish Trail and turn right (south). Follow Old Spanish Trail for a few miles until you reach the Visitors Center on the left (east) side of the street.

Phone: 520-733-5153 or 520-733-5158

Admission: $4 per vehicle, $2 for bicyclists

For a beautiful and nearby escape from the hustle and bustle of the city, Saguaro National Park East is the perfect getaway. This is a beautiful place that allows you to experience Tucson's saguaro forest and get a closer look at the desert's natural inhabitants. Located adjacent to some of Tucson's highest peaks – Rincon, Spud Rock, and the Mica

A forest of giant saguaro cacti growing near Tucson.

Julia Anderson

Mountains – it also provides some unparalleled and inspiring views.

Along the short nature trails, you're bound to spot cottontail rabbits, roadrunners, and several cactus species. If you're lucky, you may even run into a group of javelina, the Sonoran Desert's version of a wild boar. Although some people are startled by the animals, javelina generally don't bother people unless they are provoked. In the distance, you may hear coyotes howling or even see one cross your path.

For a small fee that goes to help maintain the park, you may travel the roughly paved loop that laces through the park area. Suitable for both cars and bikes, the loop is about eight miles long and offers spectacular views of the Tucson valley and the Tucson Mountains that tower over the western boundary of the city. Trails for hikers and mountain bikes are located along the side of the road. After 2-1/2 miles, you'll see the Desert Ecology Trail on the left. Along this short path, you can learn how desert plants and animals cope with their harsh environment.

Another interesting trail to follow is the Freeman Homestead Nature Trail which is only a mile long and branches off the road that's marked for the Javalina Picnic Area. As you follow the winding walkway, you can acquaint yourself with majestic saguaro cacti. Some can reach heights of more than fifty feet and often live for as many as two hundred years.

The National Park also has an interesting Visitors Center which houses exhibits of desert geology and ecology. Brief slide shows run about every half-hour, and guides lead special informational walks on some weekends in the winter.

Foremost among Arizona's many draws are its scenic desert and mountainous surroundings. Imagine finding yourself amid the countless species of plants and animals, and becoming witness to a vermilion sunset, as it stretches across the western sky. Add the dimension of riding a supple, light-footed horse through this brilliant scenario, and you may be wishing that the day wouldn't end.

If you're in search of a horseback riding experience, you needn't go far, as Tucson has several good riding stables within its boundaries. Most of them offer rides by the hour, sunset rides, hay rides, and all-day trail trips for more serious riders. Cookouts are also available, and many stables will often cater special events. While prices vary, you can expect to pay around $12 to $15 an hour for the shorter rides.

Desert-High Country Stables

Address: 6501 W. Ina Rd.

Phone: 520-744-3789

Offering a variety of options, Desert-High Country Stables offers short rides in the Tucson Mountains and Saguaro National Park West, and longer rides into the Catalina and Tortolita Mountains.

El Conquistador Stables

Address: 10000 N. Oracle Rd.

Phone: 520-742-4200

While it's located at the Sheraton Tucson El Conquistador Resort, this riding stable is open to the public. El Conquistador Stables provides trail rides in the Coronado National Forest and Santa Catalina Mountains.

Pusch Ridge Stables

Address: 13700 N. Oracle Rd.

Phone: 520-825-1664

With rides in and around the Santa Catalina Mountains, this stable offers overnight trips, moonlight rides, a summer riding school, a place to board your horse, and a host of other options for the horseback riding enthusiast.

Hiking

Hikers enjoying the view.

The mountains that surround Tucson seem to beg to be explored, and with hiking trails that can accommodate everything from a short stroll to a multi-day trip, there is something for everyone. With an elevation change of nearly 7,000 feet from the Tucson valley floor to the end of the Mt. Lemmon Highway, hiking is a four-season endeavor regardless of your level of ambition or skill. The options within one hour's drive of the city are endless and varied, and the following is just a sampling of some of the area's most spectacular trails. For more detailed information on hiking in the area, contact the Southern Arizona Hiking Club at 520-751-4531. Two outstanding hiking guides provide detailed maps and route information: Betty Leavengood's *Tucson Hiking Guide,* and the *Hiker's Guide to the Santa Ritas,* written by Leavengood with Mike Leibert.

Ed Armstorg

Hiking Trails at the Edge of the City

Romero Canyon Trail

Location: Catalina State Park

This is the northernmost hike you'll find in this book, and certainly one of the most rewarding, as Romero is the largest of the Santa Catalina range canyons. If you can get yourself to push beyond the often flowing and lovely Sutherland Wash, you'll find that the initial short pitch is steep enough to raise the heart rates of all but the fittest trekkers. From there, the trail becomes more civilized, leveling off for about a third of a mile before switch-backing its way up two more miles to the beautiful and tempting Romero Pools.

Four of the mountain ranges that surround the city of Tucson have peaks over 9,000 feet: the Santa Catalinas, Santa Ritas, Huachucas, and Chiricahuas.

Pima Canyon Trail

Location: North on First Avenue which turns into Christie.
Continue north to the end of Christie, the crossroad is Magee.
Make a right on Magee, the trailhead is at the road's end.

Beginning in the westernmost arm of the Catalinas, this popular trail offers easy access and scenic beauty to young and old alike. The trip from the 40-car paved parking lot to Pusch Ridge is a pleasant 3.2 mile jaunt that rises 900 feet in elevation and ends at a small dam. Most hikers in the area make this their turning point, leaving the upper canyon to the desert bighorn sheep, as the trail begins to take a decidedly more vertical approach and to zig-zag up the canyon walls. For the more serious hiker, a seven-mile climb to Mt. Kimball (7,200 feet) affords a view of the entire Tucson area and beyond.

Pontatoc Ridge Trail

Location: Skyline Drive to dead end of Alvernon Way.

Finding this trail can be tricky, but exploring the area here is wonderful. If you get tired of searching for the actual trail, follow the heels of someone who knows, or purchase a compass and hiking guidebook. Otherwise, work your way through the maze toward the ridge that rises to the northeast. If it has rained recently, or if there has been some substantial snowmelt, another option is to walk toward the cliffs about a half-mile to the east of the parking area for some classic desert canyon swimming.

The Cactus Forest Trail

Location: Less than one mile from the easternmost end of Broadway Blvd.

The main attractions here are the thousands of cacti that surround this trail in the foothills of the Rincons. Unlike most of the canyon hikes in the area, there are no big switchbacks. The views are more of the botanical variety. If you have negotiated the seemingly endless options and found your way to Cactus Forest Drive, you will have put just under two miles of hiking under your belt. As an "out and back," this hike can stretch for over 11 miles, but the final length of the hike is up to you.

The King Canyon Trail

Location: 0.1 miles north of the entrance to the Arizona-Sonora Desert Museum on Kinney Rd.

The King Canyon trail is the shortest of two possible routes which eventually wind to the top of Wasson Peak (4,687 feet) via the Hugh Norris Trail near the summit. The hike, which initially starts on an old jeep road, is a moderate, four-mile trek that climbs just over 1,800 feet on clearly marked trails. Among the curiosities of this trail are the several fenced-in mining shafts that were excavated in 1917 by those in search of copper.

If you don't feel like making the journey to the summit, there is a nice picnic area, the Mam-a-Gah, complete with tables and well maintained restrooms, one mile into the trail. Just west of the picnic area, along the walls of the wash, are Hohokam Petroglyphs drawn around 900-1300 A.D.

Hikes Above Tucson

The Old Baldy Trail

Location: I-19 south of Green Valley, follow the signs to Madera Canyon.

Old Baldy, also referred to as the Mt. Wrightson Trail, winds its way to a lofty 9,453 foot summit. The hike to the summit begins at the end of the Madera Canyon road, which is already 3,000 feet higher than Tucson. Winding five and a half steep miles for an additional elevation gain of about 3,700 feet, this hike is considered difficult due to some extremely steep areas. Of course, if you do persevere and reach the summit, your 360° view can stretch for hundreds of beautiful miles. It is not necessary to reach the top of the summit to enjoy the Old Baldy Trail. Josephine Saddle is just 2.2 miles up the trail and offers scenic views of Green Valley and Mt. Wrightson's peak. For a leisurely stroll, the oak trees that mark the beginning of the trail offer shade and many possibilities for picnics.

The Aspen Trail

Location: Follow the Catalina Highway to the dead end a mile beyond Summerhaven.

There are probably as many hikes off of the Catalina Highway as there are curves on the road. However, perhaps none are as cool and shady as the Aspen Trail. At around 8,000 feet, this hike can be the day-saver for the late-sleeping, warm season, Tucson area hiker. When combined with the Marshall Gulch Trail, one can loop for just under four refreshing, sometimes demanding, miles.

Birding

Known to avid birders throughout the world, the Sonoran Desert and its mountain ranges in the southeastern quadrant of Arizona offer sanctuary to as many as 450 species of birds throughout the year. It's difficult to imagine such diversity in a desert setting but, due to climatic and geological conditions, the Sonoran Desert allows for an unusually long nesting season and is an ideal place for birds to congregate.

Birds seem to be particularly abundant in certain areas of the desert during various times of the year – the Chiricahuas, Huachucas, Santa Catalinas, and the Santa Rita Mountains are just a few of these regions. To find out about the latest birding "hot spot" or to obtain general birding information and paraphernalia, you may want to wander down to the Audubon Nature Shop. Owned and operated by the Tucson Audubon Society, this store is staffed with knowledgeable volunteers who will help you find the best birding areas, and answer any questions you may have about local birds. You can even sign up for an Audubon guided field trip if you like.

The Audubon Nature Shop is located at 300 East University Boulevard. You can reach the store at 520-629-0510 and, if you're interested in unusual or rare sightings, they also maintain a "Rare Bird Alert Hotline" at 520-798-1005.

Ramsey Canyon

This Nature Conservancy preserve is one of Arizona's best known, and with good reason. A great diversity of birds from the Great Plains, Rocky Mountains, Mexican Sierra Madre, and Sonoran Desert converge upon this spot during various times of the year, making it a prime location for those who like to observe birds. Here, you can see Western and Hepatic Tanagers, Sulpher-bellied Flycatchers, Golden Eagles, Goshawks, and Whiskered Screech Owls, among countless other distinctive species.

Ramsey Canyon is best known, however, for the large variety of Hummingbirds that frequent the canyon between April and September. With as many as 13 species of Hummingbirds inhabiting the preserve during these months, the canyon has become known as the "Hummingbird Capital of the United States." The Conservancy has set up a Hummingbird feeder area, where birders and non-birders alike can sit on benches and watch as these little birds zip from feeder to feeder, making quite a show in their small-feathered finery.

The Southern Arizona area is part of a major migratory corridor, making it one of the top birding areas in North America.

In addition to its reputation as a birdwatching mecca, the canyon also offers various trails that can make for an excellent day's hike. The scenic, but somewhat steep, Hamburg Trail offers a nice overview of Ramsey Canyon, while several shorter and lower lying trails meander through the riparian areas of Ramsey Creek.

Access to Ramsey Canyon is limited by the Nature Conservancy to help preserve the canyon environment and maintain the tranquil atmosphere that makes this place so special. With space for 14 cars in the parking lot, and no parking permitted elsewhere, reservations are required for weekend and holiday visits, and are advisable during the week.

The Conservancy has six cabins available in the canyon for those who want to stay the night, but if you find these to be booked up, the Ramsey Canyon Inn is a nice alternative. A bed and breakfast hotel, the Inn is positioned just adjacent to the preserve, and offers a comfortable atmosphere with rooms that are decorated with fine antiques. Three separate cottages are also available, though breakfast is not included with these.

For more information on the Ramsey Canyon Preserve, or to make reservations, write to Ramsey Canyon Preserve, Box 84, Hereford, AZ 85615, or call 520-378-2785. To make arrangements with the Ramsey Canyon Inn, call 520-378-3010, or write to 31 Ramsey Canyon Rd., Hereford, AZ 85615.

Madera Canyon

While Ramsey Canyon may have the largest number of species of Hummingbirds, if you're looking for sheer quantity of birds, you can't beat Madera Canyon. Just 40 miles from Tucson, it makes for an excellent day trip, and is home to such inhabitants as Bewick's Wren, the Luminescent Varied Bunting, Blue Grossbeaks, Phainopepla, Pyrrhuloxia, Summer Tanagers, Bell's Vireo, Black-throated Sparrows, Flycatchers, and many more in addition to the artful Hummingbirds.

Should you decide to stay the night, the Santa Rita Lodge, located in Madera Canyon, has eight rooms and four cabins that are frequented by visitors to the area. This lodge keeps well-filled feeders near each of the cabins, so if you aren't up to walking about, you can enjoy watching the Hummingbirds from your own covered front porch. Because of the popularity of this Lodge among birders, it is best to call far in advance for reservations. The Lodge can be reached at HC70, Box 5444, Sahuarita, AZ 85629, or by phone at 520-625-8746.

The Chiricahua Mountains

Lining the southeastern portion of Arizona, the Chiricahuas offer much more than birdwatching opportunities for visitors. With rocky peaks that rise sharply above 9,000 feet and highly unusual weather patterns, this anomalous place will entice any outdoor adventurer, birder or otherwise. See the listing for the Chiricahua Mountains in the *Day Trips* section for more details.

If it's birds that bring you to this place of wonder, your best bet is to enter the Chiricahuas from the east side, through the small town of Portal. Heading west from Portal into Cave Creek Canyon, you'll find numerous areas that allow for observation of many avian species, but the crown jewel of the region is the South Fork Trail in Cave Creek Canyon. Known as one of the most famous birding trails in the nation, you can see Hummingbirds, Western Wood Pewees, Painted Redstarts, Scott's Orioles, and a host of others. But most visitors (up to 25,000 people a year) come to catch a glimpse of the rare Trogon. With an appearance that's somewhat like that of a parrot, this colorful bird inhabits the area seasonally, from April through the summer months.

With so many areas that offer outstanding opportunities for the observation of birds, we have chosen to highlight just a few of the regions in which unusual birds can be found. In addition to those mentioned above, Mt. Lemmon and Patagonia-Sonoita also offer a nice variety of birds, and provide unique perspectives from which to enjoy some of Arizona's more spectacular scenery. You'll find more information on these areas in the *Day Trips* section of this book.

Santa Cruz River and Rillito River Parks

Directions: For the quickest directions to the city's river parks from where you are staying in Tucson, call 520-740-2690 for the Rillito River Park, and 520-791-4873 for the Santa Cruz River Park.

The two major washes that travel through Tucson are the Santa Cruz and the Rillito Rivers. Although it may not seem like it when you drive by, a visit to either of these dried-up river beds can be a fun and dramatic outing. While the washes are usually bone dry, when the weather acts up, they can be gushing with water in no time. Scenic parks and pathways – that are not immediately visible from the road – run along both washes. Provided to the public by Pima County, these well-maintained parks offer ample space to run, skate, or ride your bike.

In addition to the paved and dirt paths that line the wash, the Rillito River Park has a playground for kids, complete with all the equipment you can imagine. There are also benches and drinking fountains along the way.

The Santa Cruz River Park is home to an innovative tiled sculpture of a horny toad lizard entitled "Horned Toad," that takes you by surprise as you run along the quiet path. The "Garden of Gethsemane" – a life-sized sculptural rendition of the Last Supper set in an attractive garden – is also located in the park. If you travel just north of the Speedway Overpass, you will see Tucson's only public Frisbee golf course. These parks are centrally located in Tucson, so you don't have to travel far to reach them. They see the most traffic in the early morning, and around 6 p.m., when everyone, from business people to students to stay-at-home moms, gets out to work off the stress from a long day. A visit to one of the river parks is a perfect complement to a day of shopping or sight-seeing around the city, as they allow you to have a relaxing workout, sit on a bench to people-watch, or just enjoy the desert foliage as you stroll along.

Biking

The riding in Tucson is some of the best in the country, a fact borne out by the number of biking enthusiasts who live here. You'll find great road and off-road rides all over town. If you plan to be in the area for awhile and fear that you may exhaust the following list of possibilities, you can always call or visit a bike shop and ask for more suggestions.

Bicycles West (520-887-7770, in the northwest end), Catalina Bicycle Shop (520-326-7377, slightly northeast of downtown), and Full Cycle (520-327-3232, on the east side) are three fine shops that can give you inside information on where to ride and other things you should know about cycling in and around Tucson. They also provide great service should your bike need repairs during your stay. The Greater Arizona Bicycling Association (520-885-8807) and Southern Arizona Mountain Bike Association (520-327-3232) are some other valuable resources.

Two good cycling-specific books offer good maps and important details on roads and trails. *Mountain Biking in the Old Pueblo* by Michael Jimmerson and Jim Porter is a fairly complete guide to mountain biking trails and includes some rides you can try if you're willing to travel a little farther. Philip Varney's *Bike Tours in Southern Arizona* is an authoritative and inclusive guide to the area's best road tours.

Mountain biking in the Tucson Mountains.

Chris Gould

Mountain Biking

Whether you're an avid mountain biker, or just a beginner, you'll find many options for excellent mountain biking in Tucson. There are easy trails and technical trails, intense climbs and winding flats. The best seasons to schedule a mountain biking extravaganza are winter, spring, or fall. When summer comes, mountain bikers must limit their activities to the wee hours of the morning, before the scorching heat reaches its peak.

Tucson's terrain is strictly desert, with trails that are mostly dry and rocky. Rarely will you find the smooth, single-track roller coaster trails that are so characteristic of such places as Flagstaff, Arizona, nor will you find the ground to be forgiving when you take a spill. Because of the big rocks and shocks, you'll appreciate having some sort of suspension on your bicycle, as it will prevent you from feeling like you've been operating a jackhammer all day.

Another thing to keep in mind while riding in the desert is that flat tires are a common occurrence. Nasty cactus thorns are abundant, and even if you purchase such flat-prevention products as Slime or Mr. Tuffy's, you may still get a flat or two. Thorns present another threat. Jumping cholla, prickly pear, and other cactus species line many trails, and have been known to leave their mark on many an unsuspecting mountain biker. Whenever and wherever you ride in the desert, be aware that danger may lurk around a sharp curve. Ride carefully, and don't fall on a cactus, ever.

The following includes rides that require little travel time from the city

WEST
Starr Pass

From the west side or center of town, if you ask anyone where to find a good, close place to ride, chances are he or she will tell you about Starr Pass. Located in the Tucson Mountains next to the Starr Pass resort, this is a great place to go if you don't have the time or desire to drive to a ride. The trail is well worn and offers some fun downhills.
It is a good place for beginners who are ready to test out their skills, but can be rough in some sections. If you're a more advanced rider, there's plenty of action to be found at Starr Pass.

A good way to reach the trailhead – either by car or bike – is to go west on Anklam (called St. Mary's when you go farther east), until you reach Starr Pass Resort. Turn left into the resort and follow the road until you reach a stop sign. Turn left at the stop sign, then take a right on the dirt road that's just past the intersection. Stay to the right at the fork. Follow the road until it leads you to the trailhead, and go through the entrance gate. Continue straight ahead; do not take the Yetman Trail that goes off to the right.

Once you're on the trail, follow the signs to Starr Pass. It will lead you over the Pass and then down behind a neighborhood where you can gaze at the backside of Gates Pass. Then the trail loops back around through a wash and connects up to the beginning again. Should you get temporarily lost in the series of trails, there are always other riders in the area who can help you find your way. Just be sure you bring lots of water and food. The loop ride takes about two hours and provides a nice quick cycling fix.

EAST
Saguaro National Park East

Although federal law has deemed mountain biking illegal in most national park areas, the officials at the East Park have kept one singletrack open for bikers on a trial basis. So far, the Cactus Forest Trail has remained open, as most mountain bikers have taken seriously their responsibility to accommodate hikers.

The Cactus Forest Trail is short, but extremely beautiful. To reach the entrance, take Broadway east to Old Spanish Trail and then head south until you see the entrance to the Park on your left. Maps for the trail are available at the entrance gate. Also, keep in mind that there is a $2 fee for bikes to enter the Park area.

Chiva Falls

Located east of Tucson in the Rincon Mountains, this is an extremely popular place among both mountain bikers and four-wheel-drive enthusiasts. If you prefer not to encounter Jeeps and ATCs, make sure you don't do this ride on a weekend.

The riding here is mostly on Jeep roads, very technical, and extremely rocky. If you're fairly adept, be prepared to test your skills, and if you're a beginner, you may have to carry your bike now and then. To reach the trailhead, go to the end of Tanque Verde Road. Continue east on this road, which will eventually turn into the dirt Reddington Road. You can park either at a lower parking lot and climb up a few miles to the trailhead, or in an area right at the trailhead. When deciding where to park, keep in mind that the swift downhill return on Reddington Road can be a nice way to end the ride. The views are incredible and the road is fast.

The trailhead is located 4.5 miles up Reddington Road on the right, just beyond a cattle guard. Go into the parking lot on the right and you will find the trailhead on the north end of the lot. The first downhill can be either brutal or exhilarating depending on your attitude and level of expertise. When you reach the first junction with another road, continue right. When you get to the cattle guard, veer left. At the next junction, veer right. Then cross the wash that is often running with water in the spring. At the next fork, the road goes off to the right, but stay left to go to the falls. The total distance to the falls is 4.3 miles, and intermediate to expert riders should allow about 2 hours to get there and back.

If you don't want to return the way you went to falls, you can head back to the parking lot by hooking up with Reddington Road at a higher point. Once you're at the falls, just turn around and cross the wash again. Stay left at the first junction and then go right after the cattle guard. Then turn left at Reddington Road.

Road Biking

Road biking near the Catalina Mountains.

Chris Gould

Saguaro National Park East and Old Spanish Trail Ride

This is one of Tucson's most popular rides, and is a good tour if you're a beginning rider looking to improve your performance. You can park your car at the corner of Broadway Boulevard and the Old Spanish Trail to reach this 19-mile ride, which leads you through a short 9-mile loop around Saguaro National Park East and back.

The first part of this trek is a steady climb (290 feet) along the Old Spanish Trail, all the way to the entrance of the park (5.9 miles). As you enter the park, you will pay a $2 fee, but the great scenery and wide variety of wildlife that inhabits the park make it well worth the nominal price. Catering to cyclists, the park has installed a special ramada complete with bike racks, drinking water, and benches on which you can rest or get ready for your ride.

As you approach the first steep downhill, beware that there is a sharp right turn at the bottom that has landed many a speeding rider on his or her head. Be careful. From there, you will come across several roller coaster-like hills that will level out. About halfway around the loop, you'll encounter a couple of rigorous climbs followed by more short hills. Turn right at the first stop sign. Eventually, you will come to a second stop sign and find yourself near the entrance of the park. Turning left will lead you out of the park and back onto Old Spanish Trail, where you'll have an easy downhill ride back to Broadway Boulevard.

The Colossal Cave Loop

The Colossal Cave loop is really just an extension of the Saguaro National Park East and Old Spanish Trail Ride. Instead of, or in addition to, the Saguaro National Park loop, you can continue along the Old Spanish Trail as it makes its way to Colossal Cave. This loop is a 38-mile ride, if you don't include the trip through Saguaro National Park.

As you ride past Saguaro National Park East, the grade increases slightly and maintains a steady climb, with few places along the way to catch your breath. Approximately eight miles past the park you will hit some nice rolling hills before you'll make the final ascent up to Colossal Cave. The climb from the entrance to the Visitors Center is

a steep, one-mile haul, which you may want to forgo depending on your level of conditioning. When you reach the parking lot, you can either turn around and head back or park your bike. No bikes are allowed past the parking lot. There are bike racks onto which you can lock your bike if you want to grab a snack, use the restroom, or even take the 40-minute tour of the cool and extraordinary caves.

The ride back is quick, and you should pay particular attention to the cross-traffic near the entrance to Colossal Cave, especially on the weekends.

Sabino Canyon Trail

Sabino Canyon is one of those rare areas in Arizona where the wilderness seems especially abundant and profound. The eight-mile trek can sometimes bring the rider within mere feet of the desert's many creatures that reside in the park. For more information on Sabino Canyon, see its listing under "Hiking" found earlier in this section, and in the *Attractions* section of the book.

In planning a ride in Sabino Canyon, you must take

into consideration that there are strict rules as to when you can ride in the park. While the canyon is open to visitors from dawn to dusk, bicycling is allowed only during the hours before 9 a.m. and after 5 p.m., due to the large number of people who explore the area on foot throughout the day.

Depending on what time of year you ride, the 4-mile trek to the end of Sabino Canyon can be inhibited by the overflow of water from any one of the nine bridges that crosses Sabino Creek, though most of the year this is not a problem. While the ride is all uphill to the end of the park, it's really only the last mile that becomes prohibitively steep, and you may want to turn around at this point. Coming back down, you may be tempted to let your speed build, but please note that a posted 15 m.p.h. speed limit is enforced in the park for the safety of all.

The Rancho Vistoso and Catalina Ride

The 32-mile ride to Rancho Vistoso and Catalina is one of the easier rides in the Tucson area. While there are hills, they vary from moderate to mild, making it less difficult for beginning riders or those who haven't ridden in awhile. Two other nice features of this ride are the wide shoulder areas and relatively light traffic on the roads.

This particular tour starts at the corner of Oracle and Magee Roads, where it's easy to find a place to park your car. After passing the El Conquistador Resort hotel (3.7 miles) and dipping down into the Cañada del Oro wash, look for First Avenue and turn left. Continue northward past Tangerine Road; this will take you into the retirement area of Rancho Vistoso. The road has a gentle climb and curve to it and eventually levels off and drops back around to Oracle Road (11.8 miles). At this point, you can head back down Oracle and call it a day if you like, or, continue northward on Oracle to Catalina. If you go the 4. 2 miles to Catalina, you can stop and have breakfast or lunch at Claire's Cafe. From there, you can retrace your tracks back through Rancho Vistoso (32 miles), or continue south straight down Oracle (28 miles) back to Magee.

Tucson is a dream town for climbers. Over the last two decades, the area has gained popularity on the southern swing of the international climbing circuit. Already one of the best winter climbing in the nation, Tucson has both desert routes and high-altitude routes, making it a premier climbing spot regardless of the season.

Tucson has short, bolted "sport" routes, sustained multi-pitched routes, and even multi-day aid routes. Not only is the sheer quantity of rock great, the quality of rock is excellent. Whether you seek climbs convenient to the asphalt, the solitude of seldom-seen crags in the backcountry, or even indoor climbing at the rock gyms, Tucson has what it takes to make a rockclimber skip school, ruin a relationship, or abandon a careeer.

Equipment and Guidebooks

Rock climbing in the Santa Catalinas.

Most pitches around Tucson are less than 150 feet, so the standard 50 meter rope will meet your needs. On wandering routes, double ropes are helpful. If you're climbing with a single rope, beware of rappel descents that require two ropes.

Many climbs, especially the more difficult lines in the Windy Point Vista area, are fully bolted, but it is best to refer to a more comprehensive rock climbing guidebook when more equipment is needed. Two books that are especially helpful are: *Squeezing the Lemmon: A Rock Climber's Guide to the Mt. Lemmon Highway,* by Eric-Fazio Rhicard, and *Backcountry Rockclimbing in Southern Arizona,* by Bob Kerry. Also, check the local quarterly magazine, *Desert Skies,* that's available free in shops around Tucson. Both books, and the magazine, are available at Summit Hut, and Bob's Bargain Barn, two local outdoor outfitters. Look for their addresses and phone numbers in the *Shopping* section of this book.

Safety

An important note about safety: climbing is an inherently dangerous sport, and there's no substitute for experience and good judgment. Many of the climbs in Southern Arizona are serious undertakings, and can harbor loose rock and other hazards. Wear a helmet. Think twice about trusting your life to an old fixed pro. Routes that don't receive much sun get cold quickly, especially in the windy weather, so be sure to pack warm clothing. Rain garments are a must on long routes during the summer monsoon season; do not be fooled into carelessness by clear morning skies. Difficult approaches can take more time than you expect. Be sure to take a headlamp when attempting long routes for the first time, and most importantly, don't forget to bring more water than you think you'll need.

Where to Climb

The Santa Catalinas

The Santa Catalinas, dominate the skyline north of Tucson. Rising from the cacti and desert shrub of the Tucson basin, the range tops out in the spruce and firs of the Canadian life-zone of the summit peak, Mt. Lemmon, at 9,157 feet. Over 800 established routes lie within a short distance of the two-lane paved road, the Catalina Highway, that winds to the summit. The Windy Point overlook area (a.k.a. Windy Point Vista), just past milepost 14, has the highest concentration of climbs on the mountain, with more than 150 routes within a 15-minute walk of the parking area. When it's a real scorcher down in the desert, head up to the Reef of Rocks, where it's cool. Extending north from Mt. Lemmon, the Reef of Rocks is a two-mile-long series of generally west-facing slabs and domes. The Reef's three 500-foot buttresses, collectively known as the Sea Gods, provide the highest concentration of multi-pitch routes in the Catalinas. Temperature limits the climbing season here to the period from early May to late Ocotober.

There are numerous places to camp in the Catalinas; if you don't see a "No Camping" sign you can make camp anywhere. If you're climbing at the Windy Point area and want to car camp, head down to the General Hitchcock Campground just two miles below. A good place to camp in warm weather, Hitchcock is tucked into a small area off a hairpin turn and stays in the shade most of the day. In the winter, you can catch sun by staying lower on the mountain at the Molino Basin campground just above milepost 5.

Southern Arizona Backcountry/Dragoons

The Southern Arizona backcountry has an abundance of great climbs within two hour's drive of Tucson. The driving times and foot approaches to these climbs vary greatly, but all of the areas have their individual appeal. The season and difficulty of approach will help you decide where to climb.

To get an initial taste of Southern Arizona's backcountry climbs, head east from Tucson to the Dragoon Mountains. This area of majestic spires and rugged canyons is where Cochise and the Chiricahua Apache sought refuge from the U.S. Cavalry. The Dragoons offer good car camping, hiking, and backpacking, so your non-climbing friends can soak in the scenery while you scout the approaches and climbs.

In the Dragoons you'll find three distinct climbing areas: Cochise Stronghold East, the West Stronghold, and the Sheepshead area on the south. The elevations of the climbs range from 4,500 to 6,500 feet, and since they stay warmer than the Catalinas' Windy Point Area, they're usually climbable in the winter. To get to the East Stronghold, take I-10 east from Tucson to Highway 191. Head south to Sunsites, turn right (west) on the signed road to Cochise Stronghold. The Forest Service's Coronado National Forest Chiricahua District map is ideal for this trip. The climbs and approaches are described in detail in Bob Kerry's *Backcountry Rockclimbing* guide.

Indoor Climbing Gyms

The popularity of indoor climbing continues to grow at an astonishing rate. Whereas climbers used to get their first taste of climbing out on the rock when some climbing friend, desperate for a belayer, would drag them up the mountain, it is now more likely that beginners will first climb indoors. Even the hard-core backcountry types hit the rock gyms for a quick fix in periods of bad weather. Tucson has two rock gyms: Rocks and Ropes and The Wall.

Rocks and Ropes

Address: 330 S. Toole Ave.

Phone: 520-882-5924

Hours: Weekdays 3 p.m. to 10 p.m., Weekends 11 a.m. to 8 p.m.

Rates: $5/day bouldering only, $8/day full gym, $24/day full gym, all equipment, and beginners' instruction.

Rocks and Ropes is Tucson's premier rock gym, with between 50 to 60 routes active on any given day. The beginner and warm-up routes are changed weekly, and the most difficult routes turn over about every three weeks. In addition to the top-rope climbs, the facility offers a lead area and 12-foot-high, 2,000 square foot bouldering area. There is also a pro shop and a full locker room.

The Wall Climbing Gym*

Address: 2538 N. Country Club Rd.

Phone: 520-323-6496

Hours: M-F 3 p.m. to 10 p.m.; Saturday 10 a.m. to 8 p.m.; Sunday 12 p.m. to 7 p.m.

Rates: $5/day (includes all gear). Group discounts available.

The Wall is located inside the Gymnastics Factory of Tucson, and, as the name implies, is just one wall. The 13 routes are changed monthly.

*As of press time, *The Wall Climbing Gym* is no longer open.

Skiing

Directions: Take Tanque Verde East to Catalina Highway. Turn left on Catalina Highway and drive about 30 miles to the ski area.

Mt. Lemmon Ski Valley (520-576-1400) is the closest place for the skiers of Tucson to let off some steam. There are three lifts, two of which are for beginners and the other for the more advanced skiers. The slopes are best suited for either novice skiers or those that want speed. Lemmon Drop is a must for skiers in the latter category. Since this challenging trail runs directly under the lift, it can also provide some wild entertainment for those riding up to the peak.

You can rent skis, boots, and poles at the ski area itself, or at Peter Glenn Ski & Sports (520-745-4514). Daily lift tickets cost approximately $25 for adults and $10 for people 12 and under. Private and group lessons are also available for a reasonable fee. The Iron Door Restaurant, at the base of Ski Valley, serves hearty lunches and skiers' snacks.

If you're looking for more varied terrain, head up to Snowbowl (520-779-1951) near Flagstaff, an easy five-hour drive up Interstate 10. A closer option – with even more runs – is Sunrise Ski Area (520-735-7669) in the White Mountains, which are just four hours north of Tucson.

For information on restaurants and attractions en route to Mt. Lemmon Ski Valley, see the listing for Mt. Lemmon in the *Day Trips* section of this book.

Tours

If you'd prefer to have a professional organize part or all of your sightseeing in Tucson, there are a number of experienced companies that can help. The list below is just a few of the many tour guides available that offer informative and interesting tours in and around Tucson.

Center for Desert Archaeology

Address: 3975 N. Tucson Blvd.

Phone: 520-881-2244

Contact: Connie Allen Bacon

Remarks: Reservations required.

The Center for Desert Archaeology is a non-profit organization that specializes in the study of the history and archaeology of desert regions. They offer both half-day and full-day tours that include such things as trips to the sites of petroglyphs left by the Hohokam Indians about 900 years ago.

Ajo Stage Line

Phone: 1-800-942-1981

Contact: Will Nelson

Remarks: Reservations required.

Will Nelson conducts small expeditions that can be customized to suit your personal interests. His offerings include tours to Puerto Peñasco, Mexico, the Kino missions, or Kitt Peak. He is presently the only guide that will take you to the fascinating El Pinacate volcanic area that lies just north of Puerto Peñasco. *(See listing for Puerto Peñasco in the Day Trips section of this book for more details on this area.)*

Have Fun Will Travel

Address: 11151 W. Anthony Dr.

Phone: 520-682-8659

Contact: Deb Hume and Randy Brooks

Remarks: Reservations required.

This tour company specializes in customized individual and group travel in the Southwest. Tours range from educational excursions to team-building retreats to stress-free getaways.

Trail Dust Jeep Tours

Phone: 520-747-0323

Contact: John Polaski and Bob Quinlan

Remarks: Reservations required.

Specialty tours that are currently offered through Trail Dust Jeep Tours include the Desert Ecology Tour, Desert and Mountain Tour, Overnight Tour, Gold Panning Tour, and the Sunset Champagne Tour.

Let's Go Tours

Address: 4725 E. Sunrise Dr., Suite 351

Phone: 520-299-6647

Remarks: Reservation required.

This company offers daily morning departures from your hotel to the Arizona-Sonora Desert Museum, Old Tucson Studios, Tombstone, San Xavier, or Nogales in Sonora, Mexico, and will also design custom or combination tours.

Celestial Safari

Address: 5100 N. Sabino Foothills Dr.

Phone: 520-760-2100

Remarks: Reservations required.

This guided investigation of Arizona's night sky includes telescope viewing of comets, planets, binary stars, clouds of glowing gas, clusters of stars, dying stars, and distant galaxies. Offerings vary depending on the season, so check with organizers for current tour availability.

Tucson Tours

Phone: 520-297-2911

This company offers tours to many of the region's most popular attractions, including the Arizona-Sonora Desert Museum, Old Tucson Studios, Tucson City, Mission San Xavier del Bac, Sabino Canyon, Biosphere 2, Tubac, Tombstone and Bisbee, Sedona, Nogales, Mexico, and the Grand Canyon.

Desert View Tours

Phone: 520-887-6933

Desert View will arrange visits to Arizona-Sonora Desert Museum, Old Tucson Studios, Mission San Xavier del Bac, Sabino Canyon, Biosphere 2, Tubac, Tombstone and Bisbee, and Mt. Lemmon.

Getaway Adventure Driving Tour

Phone: 1-800-288-3861

For those who prefer the flexibility of self-guided exploration, The Getaway Adventure Driving Tour can be picked up at many local bookstores or by calling the above number. The tour is comprised of a series of cassette tapes narrated by Rex Allen for such areas as Bisbee, Tombstone, Sierra Vista, and Sonoita. With these tapes, you can listen as Allen describes events and anecdotes that characterize each of these places. Included with the cassettes is a brochure that provides additional information on meals, lodging, and shopping available in the area.

Annual Events

Listed below are a number of the many interesting fiestas, fairs, sporting and cultural events that take place throughout the year in Southern Arizona. For a more complete schedule, and current dates of the events, pick up a free copy of the Tucson Official Visitors Guide at the Metropolitan Tucson Convention and Visitors Bureau at 130 S. Scott Ave., Tucson, AZ 85701, 520-624-1817.

January

Northern Telecom Open

$1.25 million tournament involving 156 professional players. Held at Tucson National Golf & Conference Resort and Starr Pass Golf Club. *520-571-0400* or *1-800-882-7660.*

Doubletree Copperbowl Adult Tennis Open

Randolph Tennis Center. *520-791-4896.*

Southern Arizona Square & Round Dance & Clogging Festival

More than 3,000 dancers participate. Tucson Convention Center. *520-885-5032.*

Tucson Marathon & Relay

1,000 runners participate in this marathon run through the city. *520-326-9383.*

Tucson Quilters Guild Show

Show includes hundreds of items, including more than 100 quilts. Tucson Convention Center. *520-791-4101*

Wings Over Willcox

Honoring the sandhill crane with birding tours, trade show, seminars, workshops.Willcox. *520-384-2272.*

February

Tucson Gem & Mineral Show

Gem, mineral, fossil, jewelry, lapidary dealers, and displays from museums worldwide. Seminars, children's program. Tucson Convention Center. *520-322-5773.*

World of Wheels Car Show

Tucson Convention Center. *520-791-4266.*

La Reunion de El Fuerte

Fort Lowell neighborhood history walk. Fort Lowell Park. *520-885-3832.*

Indian Arts Benefit Fair

Crafts, entertainment, foods. Old Town Artisans. *520-623-6024.*

Arizona All Pro Alumni Baseball Game

University of Arizona vs. UA alumni who play professionally. UA Frank Sancet Field. *520-621-4102.*

Arts & Crafts Fair

Reid Park. *520-791-4063.*

Fiddler's Contest

Bluegrass performances and competition. Reid Park.
520-791-4079.

Tucson Rodeo Parade

World's largest non-motorized parade celebrates La Fiesta
de los Vaqueros. Around Tucson Rodeo Grounds.
520-741-2233.

La Fiesta de los Vaqueros

PRCA-sanctioned, largest outdoor mid-winter rodeo in
America. Tucson Rodeo Grounds. *520-741-2233.*

Cowboy Poets Gathering

Cochise College, Sierra Vista. *520-458-7922.*

Spring

Plaza Suite

Outdoor jazz
concerts.
St. Philip's Plaza.
520-743-3399.

Tour of the Tucson Mountains

Sunday after
Easter. 1,000
cyclists tour 100
or 50 kilometer
routes around
the Tucson
Mountains.
520-745-2033.

Festival of the Arts

Exibits by North American artist and artisans. Tubac.
520-398-3269.

March

Colorado Rockies Spring Training

Pre-season major league baseball. Hi Corbett Field.
520-791-4266.

Navajo Rug & Jewelry Show, Sale, Auction

The Westin La Paloma. *520-325-6883.*

Wa:k Pow Wow

Tohono O'odham celebrate with fiddlers contest and inter-
tribal dancing. Mission San Xavier del Bac. *520-294-5727.*

Ski Carnival

Slalom, giant slalom, and mogul competition. Mt. Lemmon
Ski Valley. *520-576-1321.*

Arizona Jazz Week

University of Arizona ensembles and guest artists.
520-621-1341.

PING/Welch's Championship

More than 140 world-class golfers compete in $425,000
LPGA tournament. Randolph North Golf Course.
520-791-5742.

Tucson Toros

Houston Astros'
minor league
team.
Hi Corbett Field.
520-325-2521.

**Summerset
Suite**

Outdoor jazz con-
certs. Plaza of the
Pioneers, Tucson
Museum of Art.
520-743-3399.

**Arizona
Symphonic
Winds**

Udall Park.
520-791-4079.

European Fair

Exhibits, food, entertainment. Park Mall. *520-624-4360.*

Arts & Crafts Fair

Fort Lowell Park. *520-791-4063.*

A Celebration of Gardens

Sale of drought-tolerant plants, wildflowers, cacti, succulents, orchids, bromeliads, expert advise, tour of five home
gardens. Tucson Botanical Gardens. *520-326-9255.*

4th Avenue Street Fair

Artisans and entertainers from around the U.S.
N. Fourth Ave. between University Blvd. and E. 8 St.
520-624-5004.

April

"Simon Peter" Passion Plays

Three hour professional musical stage drama with
100-plus-member cast and orchestra. Tucson Convention
Center Music Hall. *520-327-5560.*

O'odham Arts Festival

Traditional and contemporary Native American arts and crafts for display and sale. *520-383-2221.*

Spring Fling

Food, rides, games, entertainment. University of Arizona. *520-621-5610.*

Yaqui Easter Lenten Ceremony

Ceremony combining Yaqui Indian traditions and Christian beliefs in dramatization form. Old Pascua Village. *520-791-4609.*

Horse Shows

Grand Canyon Classic Appaloosa Horse, SAAHA Spring Jubilee Horse. Pima County Fairgrounds. *520-762-9100.*

Music Under the Stars

Tucson Pops Orchestra. Reid Park. *520-791-4079.*

Concierto Qué Tal

Traditional and popular Mexican music. Reid Park. *520-791-4079.*

CIGNA Beau Bridges Celebrity Tennis Classic

Largest U.S. celebrity tennis tournament. Randolph Tennis Center. *520-623-6165.*

Pima County Fair

Carnival, livestock, exhibits, food, concerts. Pima County Fairgrounds. *520-762-9100.*

Tucson Civic Orchestra

Concert under the stars. Reid Park. *520-791-4079.*

Car Show

Pearce-Sunsites. *520-826-3378.*

Tucson International Mariachi Conference

Workshops, Garibaldi Fiesta, Mariachi showcase, two concerts, golf tournament, art exhibit. *520-884-9920 ext. 243.*

Orts Theatre of Dance

Modern dance under the stars. Reid Park. *520-791-4079.*

Gun Show

Military collectibles. Pima County Fairgrounds. *520-834-4004.*

Arts & Crafts Fair

Reid Park. *520-791-4063.*

Picnic in the Park

Dinner and music under the stars. Tohono Chul Park. *520-742-6455.*

Waila Festival

Tohono O'odham "chicken scratch" music, dancing and food. Arizona Historical Society. *520-628-5774.*

La Vuelta de Bisbee

Race of 150 top national bicyclists. Bisbee. *520-432-5421.*

Pioneer Days

Music, demonstrations, food, history re-creations of pre-statehood Arizona. Ft. Lowell Park. *520-297-5540.*

Mule Mountain Marathon

Starting from Bisbee. Sierra Vista. *520-458-6940.*

May

Tucson Arizona Boys Chorus Mother's Day Concert

Popular music and rodeo trick roping. Tucson Convention Center. *520-296-6277.*

Cinco de Mayo

Artists, music, folklorico dancers, food commemorating Mexico's victory against the French at Puebla. Kennedy Park. *520-623-8344.*

Herb Fair

Plants, sachets, gifts, teas, dried flowers, gardening advice. Tucson Botanical Gardens. *520-326-9255.*

Salute to the Buffalo Soldier

Honoring former black Army units. Sierra Vista. *520-458-6940.*

History Fest

Tours, food, entertainment, arts, crafts and period costumes. Willcox. *520-384-4376.*

Wyatt Earp Days

Gun fights, food and entertainment. Tombstone. *520-457-2211.*

Plaza Suite

Outdoor jazz concert. St. Philip's Plaza. *520-743-3399.*

Tucson Toros

Houston Astros' minor league team. Hi Corbett Field. *520-325-2621.*

Arizona Symphonic Winds

Udall Park. *520-791-4079.*

June

Music Festival

Mt. Lemmon Ski Valley. *520-576-1321.*

Juneteenth

African-American independence celebration with sports, music, food, festival. Kennedy Park Fiesta Area. *520-791-4355.*

Tucson Parks & Recreation

Community Theater, Shakespeare in the Park Classic Shakespeare under the stars. Reid Park. *520-791-4079.*

July

Independence Day

Parades, picnics, and fireworks from "A" Mountain. *520-791-4860* or *520-791-4873.*

August

Fiesta de San Augustin

Music, dancing and food honoring Tucson's patron saint. Arizona Historical Society. *520-628-5774.*

Nellie Cashman Day

Honoring the "angel of the camp" with pancake races, entertainment. Tombstone. *1-800-457-3423.*

Southwest Wings Great Birding Festival

Field trips, displays, lectures. Sierra Vista. *520-458-6940.*

Vigilante Days

Gun fights, food, fashion show, hangings. Tombstone. *1-800-457-3423.*

September

Penn Arizona Doubles Championship

Tennis tournament. Randolph Tennis Center. *520-791-4896.*

Mexican Independence Day

Music, arts, folklorico dancers, and food. Kennedy Park. *520-623-8344.*

Labor Day Golf Tournament

State's oldest continuous invitational golf tournament. Douglas. *520-364-3722.*

Brewery Gulch Days

Mining contests, tournaments, dance celebrating Bisbee's history. Bisbee. *520-432-5578.*

Rendevous of Gunfighters

Gunfighter groups throughout the U.S., costume parade. Tombstone. *1-800-457-2423.*

Music Under the Stars

Tucson Pops Orchestra. Reid Park. *520-791-4079.*

La Independencia Bike Tour

Douglas. *520-364-9410* or *520-364-4058.*

Fiesta

Mariachis, games, ballet folklorico and food. Douglas. *520-364-2477.*

Cochise County Fair

Rodeo, livestock show, music, entertainment, and food. Cochise County Fairgrounds. *520-564-5819.*

Fall

Plaza Suite

Outdoor jazz concert. St. Philip's Plaza. *520-743-3399.*

Magic Circle Bike Challenge

100, 66, and 33 mile courses. Willcox. *520-384-2995* or *520-384-3521.*

October

Jazz Sundae

Local and national musicians. Reid Park. *520-743-3399.*

Oktoberfest

German bands, dancers and food. Mt. Lemmon Ski Valley. *520-576-1321.*

Fall Plant Sale

Trees, shrubs, vines, ground covers, wildflowers, cacti, succulents, herbs, expert advice. Tucson Botanical Gardens. *520-326-9255.*

Arts & Crafts Fair

Reid Park. *520-791-4063.*

Fiesta de los Chiles

Food, plants, fine arts, crafts, clothing and jewelry. Tucson Botanical Gardens. *520-326-9686.*

Rex Allen Days

Honoring cowboy singing star Rex Allen in his hometown with parade, fair, golf tournament, rodeo and Cowboy Hall of Fame Induction. Willcox. *520-384-2272.*

KOLD-13 Cochise County Cycling Classic

Hundreds in 252, 265, 80, 30 mile courses. Cochise County perimeter. *520-745-2033.*

Art in the Park

Arts and crafts, food, entertainment. Sierra Vista. *520-458-6940.*

T.H.E. (Tucson Heritage Experience) Festival

Multicultural festival of traditional arts. El Presidio Park. *520-888-8816.*

Butterfield Overland Stage Days

Celebration of Overland mail route, re-enactment, state rides, food. Benson. *520-586-2842.*

Mineral Show

Display and sale of the world's rare minerals. Bisbee. *520-432-3500.*

Helldorado Days

Shoot-outs, parade, fashion show, street entertainment. Tombstone. *1-800-457-3423.*

Two Flags International Festival of the Arts

Exhibits, auction, parade, fun run, street fair, art show. Douglas. *520-364-1281.*

Festival of Colors

Hot air balloon festival. Sierra Vista. *520-458-6940.*

A Patagonia Affair, The Fall Festival

Food, art, crafts, dance, entertainment, walking tours. Patagonia. *520-394-2229* or *520-394-2493.*

De Anza Days

Commemorating 1775 trek of Capt. Juan De Anza to California. Tubac. *520-398-2704.*

November

Michelob Rugby Classic

Thousands of international players. Reid Park and Hi Corbett Field. *520-623-6165.*

Arts & Crafts Fair

Fort Lowell Park. *520-791-4063.*

Indian Arts Benefit Fair

Crafts, entertainment, foods. Old Town Artisans. *520-623-6024.*

Arts & Crafts Fair

Ft. Lowell Park. *520-791-4063.*

Western Music Festival

Concerts, workshops, jam sessions by top western musicians. Holiday Inn Downtown. *520-323-3311.*

Holiday In Lights

Lights, a Christmas tree, "snow," horse-drawn carriage rides, and Holiday Village. Downtown Tucson. *520-882-4040 or 520-629-9920.*

Southwestern Rockhound Roundup & Lapidary Weekend

Old Pueblo Lapidary Club rock, gem and jewelry show, exhibits, demonstrations, retailers. Rillito Park. *520-323-9145.*

Horse Shows

Arizona Paint Horse Club, All Arabian Charity, Tucson Winter Classic, Blue Ribbon Quarter Circut. Pima County Fairgrounds. *520-762-9100.*

Emmet Kelly Jr. Days

Honoring the famous clown with clown roundup, parade, contests and face painting. Tombstone. *1-800-457-4323.*

Holiday Craft Market

Music, food, arts, crafts and activities. Tucson Museum of Art. *520-624-2999.*

The Intergroup El Tour de Tucson

Thousands of cyclists in 100, 75, 50 and 25 mile races. *520-745-2033.*

Festival of Lights

Lighting Christmas decorations and arrival of Santa Claus. Nogales, Arizona. *520-287-3685.*

Christmas Apple Festival

Arts, crafts, bazaar, demonstrations, cooking contests and entertainment.Willcox. *520-584-2272.*

A Southwestern Celebration

Multi-ethnic folk festival with demonstrations and entertainment. Old Town Artisans. *520-623-5787.*

Madrigal Dinner

Renaissance holiday dinner. University of Arizona Student Union. *520-621-3546.*

Luminaria Nights

Holiday lights, music, refreshments. Tucson Botanical Gardens. *520-326-9255.*

Gun Show

Military collectibles. Pima County Fairgrounds. *520-834-4004.*

Territorial Christmas

Exhibit of more than 200 antique toys, ornaments, cards, and decorated trees. Sosa-Carrillo-Frémont House. *520-622-0956.*

Fiesta de Guadalupe

Food, music and the Posadas honoring Mexico's patron saint. De Grazia Gallery in the Sun. *520-299-9192.*

The Nutcracker Ballet

Tucson Convention Center Music Hall. *520-882-5022.*

Balloon Glo

Hot air balloons light up the night, then fly off in the morning. University of Arizona Mall. *520-888-2954.*

4th Avenue Street Fair

Artisans and entertainers from around the U.S. N. Fourth Ave. between University Blvd. and 8th St. *520-624-5004.*

Holiday Half Marathon

13.1 mile flat race. *520-326-9383.*

Tucson Marathon

Half marathon, 5K run, relay, Boston Qualifier. Oracle to Tucson. *520-326-9383.*

Tucson Arizona Boys Chorus Concert

Tucson Convention Center. *520-296-6277.*

Weiser Lock Copper Bowl

NCAA-sanctioned, Division 1 football. Arizona Stadium. *520-790-5510.*

Las Posadas

Children's procession re-enacts Mary and Joseph's search for an Inn in centuries-old Mexican tradition. Carrillo School. *520-622-6911.*

Winterhaven Festival of the Lights

Residents dress up their streets in the holiday spirit. Fort Lowell. Country Club Road. *520-327-0111.*

Christmas Apple Festival

Arts, crafts, bazaar, demonstrations, cooking contests and entertainment. Willcox. *520-584-2272.*

Tumacacori Fiesta

Celebrating cultural heritage with food, entertainment, and crafts. Tumacacori National Monument. *520-398-2704.*

Fiesta Natividad & the Festival of Lights

Luminarias and carolers. Tubac. *520-398-2704.*

Index

A

"A" Mountain 12
a.k.a. Theater 126
Adobe Rose Inn, The 92–93
Ajo Stage Line 168, 203
Allen, Rex. *See* Rex Allen
Amerind Foundation and Museum 151–152
Anna Franklin - Dolls & Marionettes 132
Anthony's in the Catalinas 67
Anthropology 43
Antigone Books 106, 117, 135
Antique Mall, The 110
Antiques and Collectibles 110–111
Apache Indians 43, 141, 154, 199
Aqui Esta 99
Archaeology 203
Arizona - Sonora Desert Museum 25–27, 55, 90, 204, 205
Arizona Children's Theatre 127
Arizona Friends of Chamber Music 130
Arizona Hatters 104
Arizona Historic Society 14, 23
Arizona Historical Society Museum 42, 91
Arizona Inn, The 67–68, 85–86,
Arizona Office of Tourism 156
Arizona Opera 130
Arizona Repertory Theatre 128
Arizona Rose Theatre 127
Arizona State Museum 12, 42–43, 54
Arizona Territorial University 13
Arizona Theatre Company 127
Arlene's Gallery 140
Armory Park Historic District 14, 21
Art Galleries 34, 49, 50, 132
Aspen Trail 184
Assistance League Thrift & Craft Shop 111
Astronomy 46–47, 48, 204
Audubon Nature Shop 184

B

B & B Cactus Farm 115
Baggin's 76
Bahti Indian Arts 103
Bailey & Bailey Café (B&B) 22, 74
Bajada Loop Drive 177, 178
Ballet Arizona 129
Balloon Glo 218
Barrio Historico 14, 19, 20, 93, 121
Bars 120–121
Bazil's 69
Bear Canyon 31
Bed and Breakfast Inns 88, 140, 149
Berky's 121
Berta Wright 100, 116
Biking 189–196, 208, 211, 214, 215, 217. *See also* Mountain Biking; Road Biking
Biosphere 2 40–41, 204, 205
Bird Cage Theatre 139
Birds 26, 32, 33, 147, 153, 167, 184, 186, 207, 213
Bisbee 141–143, 204, 205, 214
Bisbee Chamber of Commerce 143
Bisbee Mining and Historical Museum 142
Blue Willow 59
Bob's Bargain Barn 106
Boccata 61
Bond Boot Company 105
Book Mark, The 107
Booked Up 106
Bookman's 107, 117
Books West Southwest 108, 117
Bookstores 106–108
Boothill Graveyard 140
Boots 104–105
Bowling 124
Buddy's Grill 65
Buffalo Exchange 113

Buffalo Soldiers 159, 212
Bum Steer, The 120
Butterfield Stage Coach 13, 215

C

Cactus Forest Trail 182, 192
Cactus Moon 122
Cactus Nurseries 114–115
Café Magritte 59
Café Paraiso 75
Café Poca Cosa 60
Café Roka 143
Café Sweetwater 122
Café Terra Cotta 60
Callaghan Vineyards 150
Campbell Gallery 17
Canyon Cafe, Loew's Ventana 84
Canyon Ranch Resort 80–81
Capriccio Ristorante 70
Caruso's 69
Casa Alegre 92
Casa de los Niños Thrift Superstore 112
Casa Tierra 90
Cascabel Ranch 39
Casino of the Sun 124
Casinos 123–124
Catalina Park Inn 89
Catalina State Park 181
Cave Creek Canyon 187
CCC Chuckwagon Suppers 123
CEDO, Intercultural Center 168
Celestial Safari 204
Center for Creative Photography 49
Center for Desert Archaeology 203
Chile Pepper 144
Chiricahua Crest Trail 153
Chiricahua Mountains 184, 187
Chiricahua National Monument 153
Chiva Falls - Mountain Bike Ride 192–193
Circle Z Ranch 95
City Grill 66
Climate 8
Climbing. *See* Rock Climbing
Club Congress 88, 120
Coffee Houses 74–76
Colorado River Yuma Indians 43
Colorado Rockies Spring Training 208
Colossal Cave 38–39
Colossal Cave Loop - Bike Ride 194–195
Commonwealth Mine and Mill 157
Congress Hotel 120
Copper Queen Consolidated Mining Company 141
Copper Queen Hotel, The 143
Corbett House, The 18
Coronado National Memorial 158
Coronado Peak 158
Corral Western Wear 104
Courtland 156–157
Coyote's Voice Books 107
Crystal Palace Saloon 140
Cuppuccino's Coffee House 75
Cushing Street Bar and Grill 20, 121

D

Dakota Café and Catering Company 64
Dance 129, 207, 211, 218
Daniel's 70
Davis Monthan Air Force Base 13–14, 44
De Grazia's Gallery in the Sun 34–35
Desert Diamond Casino 123
Desert Discovery Nature Trail 177
Desert Ecology Trail 179
Desert Garden, La Paloma 79
Desert Golf Tours 176
Desert Son 102
Desert View Tours 205
Desert Vintage and Costume 113, 117
Desert-High Country Stables 180
Discount Agate House 116
Discovery Zone Fun Center 126

Dos Locos Cantina, El Conquistador 83
Doubletree Copperbowl Adult Tennis Open 206
Downtown Saturday Night 119
Dragoon Mountains 157, 199
Dude Ranchers Association 95
Dude Ranches 94–97
Duquesne House Bed & Breakfast 149

E

Echo Canyon 154
Edward Nye Fish House 17
18 Steps 143
El Changarro 164
El Charro 57
El Conquistador Stables 180
El Corral 64
El Fronterizo 22
El Minuto 57
El Pinacate 167, 203
El Presidio District 14, 16–19, 58
El Presidio Fortress 16
El Presidio Gallery 133
El Rio Municipal Golf Course 171
El Saguarito 57
El Sarape 164
El Tiradito. See Wishing Shrine
Elgin 150
Elvira's 165
Elysian Grove Market 93–94
Embassy Suites-Tucson/Broadway 86–87
Encore Med and Café Triana 72
Epic Café 75
Er Pastaro 150
Espero Canyon Trail 31
Etherton Gallery 133
Ethnic Arts and Decor 99

F

Family Fun 124–126
Fantasy Golf Tours 176
Father Eusebio Francisco Kino 12, 36, 146
Fiesta Lanes 124
Firehouse Antiques Center 110
Flandrau Science Center and Planetarium 48, 91
Flowers 32, 47, 52, 114
Flying V Bar and Grill, The, Loew's Ventana 84
Footprints of a Gigantic Hound 108
Fort Huachuca 158
Fort Huachuca Historical Museum 159
Fourth Avenue Merchants Association 119
Fourth Avenue Street Fair 209, 219
Francisco Vásquez de Coronado 158
Fred Enke Municipal Golf Course 171
Freeman Homestead Nature Trail 179
Frisbee Golf Course 188
Funtasticks Family Fun Park 125

G

Gadsen Purchase 13, 144
Galleries. See Art Galleries
Gallery in the Sun Museum 34
Garden of Gethsemane 188
Gaslight Theatre 127
Gates Pass 27, 177–178
General Hitchcock Campground 161, 199
Gentle Ben's Brewing Company 121
Geronimo 154, 159
Gertrude's Collectibles 110, 116
Getaway Adventure Driving Tour 205
Ghost Towns 156–157
Gleeson 156
Gold Room, Westward Look 82
Golden Pin Lanes 124
Golf 171–175, 206, 209, 214
Golf and Stuff 125
Golf Tours 176
Graycie's Gift & Candle Shop 148
Great Western Mining Company 156
Greater Arizona Bicycling Association 189
Guevavi. See Mission Los Angeles de Guevavi

H

Hailstone Trail 154
Hamburg Trail 185
Haunted Bookshop, The 108
Have Fun Will Travel 203
High Desert Inn, The 143
Hiking 177, 181–184
Historic Block 14, 50
Historic Downtown 14–16
Hohokam Indians 12, 30, 144
Hohokam Petroglyphs 183, 203
Holiday In Lights 217
Hon Dah House 140
Honky Tonks and Western Clubs 122–123
Hopi Indians 43
Horse Shows 210, 217
Horseback Riding 180
Hotel Congress 87–88
Hotel Plaza Las Glorias 168
How Sweet it Was 114, 117
Huachuca Mountains 158, 184
Hugh Norris Trail 177, 183
Hummingbirds 26, 147, 149, 185, 186

I

Indian Territory 102
Indoor Climbing Gyms 200
Intergroup El Tour de Tucson 217
International Wildlife Museum 41
Invisible Theatre 128
Iron Door Restaurant 161, 201
Ironwood Terraces 27

J

Janos 18, 62–63
javelina 179
Jeff's Classical Records 109, 117
John & Sandy's Rattlesnake & Apache Crafts 156
Johnson Peak 154
Juan Bautista de Anza National Historic Trail 145

K

Kachina dolls 29, 102
Kaibab Shops 102, 117
Karen's Wine Country Café 150
Keaton's 66
Kimball Springs Café and Bakery 161
King Canyon Trail, The 183
Kingfisher 64
Kino, Fr. Eusebio. See Father Eusebio Francisco Kino
Kitt Peak 46–47, 203

L

La Casa Cordova 17, 101
La Fuente 58
La Montura 145
La Paloma Dining Room 80
La Placita Café 58
La Posada Del Valle 90–91
La Posta Quemada Ranch 38
La Roca 165
La Villa's, La Paloma 79
La Vista, El Conquistador 83
Lake Patagonia 148
Land of the Standing-Up Rocks, The 153
Las Brasas 164
Last Territory Steakhouse, El Conquistador 83
Lavender Pit Open Mine Bus Tour 142
Lazy Frog 163
Lazy K Bar Ranch 95–96
Le Bistro 71
Le Rendez-vous 72
Let's Go Tours 204
L'il Abner's Steakhouse 63
Little Bit of Texas 123
Little House 149
Lodging in Bisbee 143
Lodging in Patagonia 149
Lodging in Ramsey Canyon 186
Lodging in Rocky Point 168
Loews Ventana Canyon Resort 83–84, 172

Lookout Bar & Grille, Westward Look 82
Lotus Garden 73
Lucky Strike Bowl 124

M

Madera Canyon 186
Madera Designs 99
Magellan Trading 100
Mam-a-Gah Picnic Area 183
Maps 10, 11, 15, 16, 20, 21, 54, 55, 116, 117, 137, 157
Mariachi 59, 83, 210, 214
Mariachi Mass 23
Marshall Gulch Trail 184
Massai Point 154
Maverick, King of Clubs 122
Mesquite Grove Gallery 148
Mexican Food 27, 57–59, 164–165
Mexican Heritage Museum 17
Mexico - Car Insurance 166
Mexico - Nogales, Puerto Peñasco 162–169
Mi Nidito 58
Milagro 76
Mines, Mining 13, 42, 139–140, 141–142, 142–143, 156–157
Mission Los Angeles de Guevavi 146
Mission San Xavier del Bac 36–37, 204, 205
Missions 36, 146
Molino Basin 161, 199
Monsoon 9
Monte Vista Peak 154
Morning Star Traders 101
Morse Canyon Trailhead 154
Mountain Biking 190–191
Mt. Kimball 182
Mt. Lemmon 93, 160–161, 187, 198, 205
Mt. Lemmon Cafe 161
Mt. Lemmon Ski Valley 160, 201
Mt. Wrightson 147
Mt. Wrightson Trail 183
Mule Mountains 141
Mulheim Heritage House Museum 142
Murals 134
Museum of the West 139
Museums 14
Music, Live 130–131, 208–212, 214, 217, 219
Music Stores 109

N

Nacimientos 17, 162
National Optical Astronomy Observatories (NOAO) 46
Nature Conservancy 147, 185
Navajo Indians 43, 151, 208
Nightclubs 120–121
Nogales 162–165, 204
Northern Telecom Open 174, 206

O

O.K. Corral 139
Obsidian Gallery 133
Ocumicho Indians 163
Oktoberfest 215
Old Baldy Trail 183
Old Pueblo Trolley 54
Old Spanish Trail Ride 194
Old Territorial Bookstore 42
Old Town Artisans 19, 101, 116
Old Tucson Studios 13, 28, 204, 205
Olive Tree 72
O'odham Arts Festival 210
Organ Pipe National Monument 167
Orts Theatre of Dance 129, 211
Outdoor Gear 105–106
Ovens of Patagonia, The 148
Ovens Restaurant 61

P

Padre Eusebio Francisco Kino. See Father Eusebio Francisco Kino
Park Mall 98
Parker Canyon Lake 148

Patagonia 147–149, 187, 216
Patagonia Gallery 148
Patagonia Mountains 147
Patagonia Sonoita Creek Preserve 147
PDQ Records and Tapes 109
Pearce 157
Penn Arizona Championship 213
Peppertrees Bed and Breakfast Inn 91
Petroglyphs. See Hohokam Petroglyphs
Phelps Dodge 141
Philabaum Contemporary Art Glass 134
Photography. See Center for Creative Photography
Picante Designs 100, 116
Picnics 30, 39, 47, 145, 148, 149, 151, 177, 179, 183
Pima Air and Space Museum 14, 43–45
Pima Canyon Trail 182
Pima County Courthouse 19
Pima County Fair 210
Pima Indians 144
PING Welch's LPGA Open 172, 209
Pinnacle Peak 63
Pontatoc Ridge Trail 182
Portal 187
Presidio Grill 65
Presidio Museum, The 144
Pronto 76
Puerto Peñasco 165–169
Pusch Ridge 182
Pusch Ridge Stables 180

Q

Queen Mine Tour 141
Quinlan Mountains 46

R

Rainfall 9
Ramsey Canyon Inn 186
Ramsey Canyon Preserve 185
Rancho Vistoso and Catalina Ride 196
Randolph Municipal Golf Courses 172
Rare Bird Alert Hotline 184
Rattlesnake Canyon 31
Red Hills Visitors Center 178
Red Mountain Foods 149
Reddington Land & Cattle Company 39
Reid Park Zoo 29
Resorts 79–85
Rex Allen 155, 215
Rex Allen Museum 155
Rhyolite Canyon 154
Rillito River 188
Rillito River Park 188–189
Rimrock West Hacienda 93
Rincon Mountains 38, 96, 178, 182, 192
River Walks 188
Road Biking 194–196
Rock Climbing 197–200
Rocks and Ropes 200
Rocky Point 165–169
Romero Canyon Trail 181
Romero House 18
Romero Pools 181
Rose Canyon Lake 160
Rothrock Cottage and Adobe 149
Running 207, 211, 219
Rustica 99

S

Sabino Canyon 30–32, 93, 204, 205
Sabino Canyon Tours, Inc. 30, 32
Sabino Canyon Trail - Bike Ride 195–196
Saguaro 33
Saguaro Moon Antiques 111, 116
Saguaro National Park East 38, 88, 93, 178–179, 192, 194
Saguaro National Park West 90, 177–178, 180
Saint Augustine Cathedral 23
Sakura Teppan Steak and Sushi 73
San Augustin de Tucson 12
Sanchez Burrito Company 77

Sandy Beach 168
Santa Catalina Mountains
    79, 80, 81, 82, 96, 160, 172, 180, 181–
    182, 184, 198–199
Santa Cruz River 12, 37
Santa Cruz River Park 188–189
Santa Cruz Valley 16
Santa Cruz Winery 150
Santa Rita Country Club 173
Santa Rita Lodge 187
Santa Rita Mountains 95, 147, 173, 184
School House Inn 143
Second-Hand and Resale Boutiques 113–114
Sentinel Peak. See "A" Mountain
Seri Indians 43
Seven Falls 31
Shelter, The 120
Sheraton El Conquistador Resort and Country Club
    82–83, 173, 180
Sierra Vista 158
Silverbell Municipal Golf Course 174
Singing Wind Bookshop 151
Sinners Shrine. See Wishing Shrine
Skate Country: East and North 125
Skiing 201, 209
Sobaipuri Indians 12
Sonoita 150, 187, 205
Sonoita Vineyards 150
Sonoran Desert Marketplace 116
Sosa-Carrillo-Frémont House Museum 23
South Fork Trail 187
Southern Arizona Light Opera Company (SALOC) 128
Southern Arizona Mountain Bike Association 189
Southern Arizona Square Dance Festival 207
Southern Paiute Indians 43
Southwest Dance 130
Speedway Outlet 112
Spring Fling 210
Sprouts 74
St. Ann's Catholic Church 145
Starr Pass - Mountain Bike Ride 191–192
Starr Pass Golf Course 174
Stevens House 17
Stewart Boot Company 105
Stout Cider Mill 155
Summerhaven 161
Summit Hut 105
SunCatcher, The 88–89

T
Tack Room, The 68
Tanque Verde Greenhouses 114
Tanque Verde Mountains 96
Tanque Verde Ranch 96
Tap Room, The 121
Tarahumara Indians 43
Tea Room and Garden Café 34
Tee Time Arrangers & Tours, Inc. 176
Telephone Line Trail 31
Telescopes 46–47, 48, 204
Temperature 8
Temple of Music and Art 22
Tennis 206
Territorial Room, The 140
Theater 126–128, 210, 212
Third Street Antique Mall 140
Thrift Stores 111–112
Thursday Night ArtWalk 132
Tierra Madre 103
Titan Missile Museum 45
Tohono Chul Park 32–34, 108
Tohono O'odham
    32, 37, 43, 47, 123, 144, 146, 178, 209, 210, 211
¡Toma! 58
Tombstone 138–140, 156, 204, 205, 212, 214, 216
Tombstone Chamber of Commerce 140
Tombstone Historama 139
Tooley's Taco Stand 99
Tortolita Mountains 180
Tortuga Books 144

Trail Dust Jeep Tours 204
Trails 31, 145, 153, 154, 158, 167, 177, 179, 181–
    184, 185, 187
Trio Bistro and Bar 60
Trolley Service. See Old Pueblo Trolley
Tubac 144–146, 204, 205
Tubac Center for the Arts 146
Tubac Golf Resort 145
Tubac Presidio State Historic Park 144, 145
Tucson Arts District Partnership, Inc. 119, 132
Tucson Audubon Society 184
Tucson Botanical Gardens 52–53
Tucson Children's Museum 22, 51
Tucson Gem & Mineral Show 207
Tucson International Mariachi Conference 210
Tucson Jazz Society, The 131
Tucson Mall 98
Tucson Mountain Park 27
Tucson Mountains 28, 97, 174, 177, 180
Tucson Museum of Art 14, 17, 50–
    51, 62, 94, 101, 116
Tucson National Golf & Conference Resort 84–85
Tucson National Golf Resort 175
Tucson Quilters Guild Show 207
Tucson Rodeo Parade 208
Tucson Symphony Orchestra 131
Tucson Thrift 114, 117
Tucson Toros 209, 212
Tucson Tours 204
Tucson Visitor's Bureau 14, 206
Tucson Visitors Center 140
Tucson's Map and Flag Center 115
Tumacacori Mission 146
Tumacacori National Historical Park 146
Turquoise Door 102

U
U.S. Cavalry 154, 158, 199
UA Theatre Arts 128
Unique Antique 111
University of Arizona 14, 91
University of Arizona Museum of Art 49–50
University of Arizona UA Presents 131
Urbane Cowgirl 104, 116

V
Valley View Overlook Trail 177
Value Village 112, 117
Vegetarian 27, 74
Vineyards 150
Vivace 71

W
Waila Festival 211
Wall Climbing Gym, The 200
Wasson Peak 177, 183
Weather 8
Western Boots and Attire 104
Westin La Paloma, The 79–80
Westward Look Resort 81–82
White Dove, El Conquistador 83
White Dove of the Desert. See Mission San Xavier del
    Bac
White Stallion Ranch 97
Wild Johnny's Wagon 62
Willcox 154–155, 212
Windmill Inn at St. Philip's Plaza 87
Wine Tasting 150
Wishing Shrine 20

Y
Yaqui 43, 124, 210
Yaqui Easter Lenten Ceremony 210

Z
Zia Record Exchange 109
Zoo. See Reid Park Zoo

About the Authors

Carolyn Grossman has lived in Tucson since 1991, with her husband, Herb, and children, Jonathan and Michael. Raised on the West Coast, Carolyn loves the mountains and the desert of Tucson, and appreciates the friendly people and laid-back atmosphere for which the area is known.

Suzanne Myal has been visiting Tucson since 1967, and relocated to the city in 1988 with her husband, Mick. Since her first trip to Europe, Sue's hobby has been reading travel books, and she has traveled extensively throughout the U.S., Europe, the Caribbean, and Mexico. She has three children and five grandchildren.

Suzanne Myal and Carolyn Grossman.